DevOps Troubleshooting

DevOps Troubleshooting

Linux® Server Best Practices

Kyle Rankin

⋏⋏ Addison-Wesley

Upper Saddle River, NJ • Boston • Indianapolis • San Francisco
New York • Toronto • Montreal • London • Munich • Paris • Madrid
Capetown • Sydney • Tokyo • Singapore • Mexico City

The publisher offers excellent discounts on this book when ordered in quantity for bulk purchases or special sales, which may include electronic versions and/or custom covers and content particular to your business, training goals, marketing focus, and branding interests. For more information, please contact:

U.S. Corporate and Government Sales
(800) 382-3419
corpsales@pearsontechgroup.com

For sales outside the United States, please contact:

International Sales
international@pearson.com

Visit us on the Web: informit.com/aw

Cataloging-in-Publication Data is on file with the Library of Congress.

ISBN-13: 978-0-321-83204-7
ISBN-10:   0-321-83204-3

This product is printed digitally on demand.

First printing, November 2012

Editor-in-Chief
Mark Taub

Executive Editor
Debra Williams Cauley

Development Editor
Michael Thurston

Managing Editor
John Fuller

Project Editor
Elizabeth Ryan

Copy Editor
Rebecca Rider

Indexer
Richard Evans

Proofreader
Diane Freed

Technical Reviewer
Bill Childers

Publishing Coordinator
Kim Boedigheimer

Compositor
Kim Arney

This book wouldn't be possible without the support of my wife, Joy, who once again helped me manage my time so I could complete the book, only this time while carrying our first child, Gideon. I'd also like to dedicate this book to my son, Gideon, who so far is easier to troubleshoot than any server.

Contents

Preface

DevOps describes a world where developers, Quality Assurance (QA), and systems administrators work more closely together than in many traditional environments. Although DevOps is already recognized as a boon to rapid software deployment and automation, an often-overlooked benefit of the DevOps approach is the rapid problem solving that occurs when the whole team can collaborate to troubleshoot a problem on a system. Unfortunately, developers, QA, and sysadmins have gaps in their troubleshooting skills that they often resolve by blaming each other for problems on the system. This book aims to bridge those gaps and guide all groups through a standard set of troubleshooting practices that they can apply as a team to some of the most common Linux server problems.

Although the overall topics covered in the book are traditionally the domain of sysadmin, in a DevOps environment, developers and QA also find themselves troubleshooting network problems, setting up web servers, and diagnosing high load, even if they may not have a background in Linux administration. What makes this book more than just a sysadmin troubleshooting guide is the audience and focus. This book assumes the reader may not be a Linux sysadmin, but instead is a talented developer or QA engineer in a DevOps organization who may not have much system-level Linux experience. That said, if you are a sysadmin, you won't be left out either. Included are troubleshooting techniques that can supplement the skills of even senior sysadmin—just written in an accessible way.

In a traditional enterprise environment without DevOps principles, troubleshooting is as dysfunctional as development is. When there is a server problem, if you can even get developers and sysadmin on the same call, you can expect everyone to fall into their traditional roles—the sysadmin will only look at server resources and logs; the developers will wait for the inevitable blame to be heaped on them for their "bloated" or "buggy" code, at which point they will complain about the unstable, underpowered server; or maybe everyone will redirect the blame at QA for not finding the problem before it hit production. All the while, the actual problem is not any closer to being solved.

In a DevOps organization, cooperation between all the teams is stressed, but when it comes to troubleshooting, often people still fall into their traditional roles even if there's no blame game. Why? Well, even if everyone wants to work together, without the same troubleshooting skills and techniques, everyone may still be waiting on everyone else to troubleshoot their part. The goal of this book is to get every member of your DevOps team on the same page when it comes to Linux troubleshooting. When everyone has the same Linux troubleshooting skills, the QA team will better be able to diagnose problems before they hit production, developers will be better at tracking down why that latest check-in doubled the load on the system, and sysadmins can be more confident in their diagnoses, so when a problem strikes, everyone can pitch in to help.

This book is broken into ten chapters based on some of the most common problems you'll face on Linux systems, and the chapters are ordered so that techniques you learn in some of the earlier chapters (particularly about how to diagnose high load and how to troubleshoot network problems) can be helpful as you get further into the book. That said, I realize you may not read this book cover-to-cover, but instead you will probably just turn to the chapter that's relevant to your particular problem. So when topics in other chapters are helpful, I will point you to them.

- **Chapter 1: Troubleshooting Best Practices** Before you learn how to troubleshoot specific problems, it may be best to learn an overall approach to troubleshooting that you can apply to just about any kind of problem, even outside of Linux systems. This chapter talks about general troubleshooting principles that you will use when you try specific troubleshooting steps throughout the rest of the book.

- **Chapter 2: Why Is the Server So Slow? Running Out of CPU, RAM, and Disk I/O** This chapter introduces troubleshooting principles that you will apply to one of the most common problems you'll have to solve: Why is the server slow? Whether you are in QA and are try-ing to figure out why the latest load test is running much slower; you are a developer trying to find out if your program is I/O bound, RAM bound, or CPU bound; or you are a sysadmin who isn't sure whether a load of 8, 9, or 13 is OK, this chapter will give you all the techniques you need to solve load problems.

▨ **Chapter 3: Why Won't the System Boot? Solving Boot Problems**   Any number of different problems can stop a system from booting. Whether you have ever thought about the Linux boot process or not, this chap-ter helps you track down boot problems by first walking you through a healthy Linux boot process, and then discussing what it looks like when each stage in that boot process fails.

▨ **Chapter 4: Why Can't I Write to the Disk? Solving Full or Corrupt Disk Issues**   Just about anyone who has used Linux for a period of time has run across a system where they can't write to the disk. It could be that you are a developer who enabled debugging in your logs and you accidentally filled the disk, or you could simply be the victim of file system corruption. In either case, this chapter helps you track down what directories are using up the most space on the system and how to repair corrupted file systems.

▨ **Chapter 5: Is the Server Down? Tracking Down the Source of Net-work Problems**   No matter where you fit in a DevOps organization, network troubleshooting skills are invaluable. Sometimes it can be dif-ficult to track down networking problems because they often impact a system in strange ways. This chapter walks you through how to iso-late and diagnose a network problem step-by-step by testing problems on different network layers. This chapter also lays the groundwork for troubleshooting techniques for specific network services (such as DNS) covered in the rest of the book.

▨ **Chapter 6: Why Won't the Hostnames Resolve? Solving DNS Server Issues**   DNS can be one of the trickier services to troubleshoot because even though so much of the network relies on it, many users are unfamiliar with how it works. Whether you are a web developer who gets DNS service for your site on a web GUI via your registrar, or a sysadmin in charge of a full BIND instance, these DNS troubleshooting techniques will prove invaluable. This chapter will trace a normal, successful DNS request and then elaborate on the DNS troubleshooting covered in Chapter 5 with more specific techniques for finding problems in DNS zone transfers, caching issues, and even syntax errors.

Chapter 7: Why Didn't My Email Go Through? Tracing Email Problems   Email was one of the first services on the Internet and still is an important way to communicate. Whether you are tracing why your automated test emails aren't being sent, why your software's email notifications are stuck, or why mail delivery is down for your entire company, this chapter helps you solve a number of email problems, including misconfigured relay servers and DNS-related mail server issues. This chapter even shows you how to send an email "by hand" with telnet.

Chapter 8: Is the Website Down? Tracking Down Web Server Problems   So many of the applications we interact with on a daily basis are based on the Web. In fact, if you are a software developer, there's a good chance web programming is at least a part of what you develop, and if you are a sysadmin, you are likely responsible for at least one web server. Web server troubleshooting is a large topic, but for the purposes of this chapter, you only learn about the common problems you are likely to run into with two of the most popular web servers today: Apache and Nginx. This chapter discusses how to pull server status and how to identify the cause of high server load as well as other common debugging techniques.

Chapter 9: Why Is the Database Slow? Tracking Down Database Problems   Just like much of the software you use on a daily basis is on the Web, much of the software you use stores its data in some sort of database. This chapter is similar to Chapter 8, only its focus is on troubleshooting problems with two popular open source database servers: MySQL and PostgresSQL. As with Chapter 8, it discusses how to pull load metrics from these databases and how to identify problem queries as well as other causes of high load.

Chapter 10: It's the Hardware's Fault! Diagnosing Common Hardware Problems   With all this focus on software, we should also discuss one of the most common causes of server problems: hardware failures. The problem with hardware failures is that often hardware doesn't fail outright. Instead, segments of RAM have errors, hard drive sectors fail, or Ethernet cards drop random packets. What's worse, these failures often cause software problems that are almost impossible to track down. This chapter discusses how to troubleshoot some common hardware failures, from bad RAM, to failing hard drives, to dying network cards. This chapter contains hardware troubleshooting techniques you can apply anywhere—from a production rackmount server to your personal laptop.

Acknowledgments

THANKS TO DEBRA for advocating for this book, from the first time the idea came up all the way through to it becoming a real book. Thanks also to Trotter and Bill for all of their feedback along the way. Finally, thanks to all of the broken systems I've worked on through the years that helped me hone my troubleshooting skills.

About the Author

Kyle Rankin is a senior systems administrator and DevOps engineer; the current president of the North Bay Linux Users' Group; author of *The Official Ubuntu Server Book, Knoppix Hacks, Knoppix Pocket Reference, Linux Multimedia Hacks,* and *Ubuntu Hacks*; and a contributor to a number of other books. Rankin is an award-winning columnist for *Linux*™ *Journal* and has written for *PC Magazine*, TechTarget websites, and other publications. He speaks frequently on open source software, including at SCALE, OSCON, Linux World Expo, Penguicon, and a number of Linux Users' Groups.

## CHAPTER 1

Troubleshooting Best Practices

TROUBLESHOOTING IS A SKILL. As with all skills, whether it's juggling, playing the guitar, cooking, or programming, some people naturally have a knack for troubleshooting and others don't. If a skill comes naturally to you, you might assume it comes naturally to everyone else. After all, if you rode a bike on your first try, you may take for granted how much work other people have to put into it.

Some people are naturally good at troubleshooting. When faced with a problem, they automatically snap into action and instinctively pick steps that further isolate the problem until they have found the root cause. When you take a car to a good mechanic, one who is good at troubleshooting, right after you describe your symptoms you can see the gears turning; he's already isolated the problem to a handful of causes and has a "hunch" about the root cause. After a few tests he will have confirmed his hunch and be well on his way toward fixing your car. On the other hand when you take your car to a mechanic who's bad at troubleshooting, you can expect high repair bills and trip after trip to the shop as one after another part of your car is replaced.

Troubleshooting is a skill that anyone can learn. As with many skills, certain techniques are involved in troubleshooting that, whether they come naturally or not, can become second nature through practice. You not only want to be a better troubleshooter, you also want to be *faster*. This is especially true when you work in an environment where downtime is measured in dollars. After all, both the good mechanic and the bad mechanic will eventually fix your car, but which one would you prefer work on it?

In a DevOps organization, everyone on the team is responsible for some level of troubleshooting. A developer troubleshoots bugs in his software, a sysadmin troubleshoots problems on her hardware, and the QA team spends a great majority of their time first finding problems and then trying to locate the root cause. When everyone on the DevOps team uses the same proven troubleshooting techniques, the whole team benefits.

This chapter describes some troubleshooting best practices you can apply to just about any problem. Most of these practices are fairly common-sense once you read them, but you might be amazed how many people skip them when faced with a problem.

Divide the Problem Space

If I asked you to guess a number I was thinking of from 1 to 100, what number would you guess? Let's say the number is 73, and after every guess I will tell you whether the number is higher or lower than your guess. Some people might start randomly guessing numbers, or start with 1 and work their way up. Someone who is good at troubleshooting would probably guess something like: 50 (higher), 75 (lower), 63 (higher), 69 (higher), 72 (higher), 73. With each guess, the number of possibilities was cut in half. In this example it took 6 guesses to find the right answer, whereas if you started from 1 and went up, it would take 73. If you just guessed randomly you might go through all the numbers before you lucked into the right one.

This same approach applies to all troubleshooting. When faced with a problem, some just start at the bottom of the list of possible causes and work their way up; others choose random tests until they luck into the cause. A good troubleshooter chooses each test so that the result will rule out a class of causes, not just a single cause. Divide and conquer. When you divide the problem space, even if a test doesn't reveal the *root* cause, the results rule out more than one cause.

For instance, if I tried to load a website in my browser and the request timed out, and I wanted to test whether the problem was with their site or my Internet connection, I wouldn't immediately go to the back of my computer to make sure the Ethernet cable was plugged in. Instead I would probably try to load one or two other websites I know are usually stable. If those other websites came up, I would know my Internet connection was fine and would have just ruled out an entire set of local networking tests.

When you are problem solving with a team of people, you will also want to divide the problem space between members of the team. Nothing is worse than tracing down a problem only to find out your teammate has been working on the same exact test. When you set out to solve a problem in a team setting, assign different tests to each person and make sure that once someone has ruled out a cause, the result is communicated to everyone else.

Practice Good Communication When Collaborating

One of the biggest challenges when troubleshooting with a team is establishing good methods of communication. Without good communication, two people work on the same problem without realizing it, people go down troubleshooting paths that someone else has already ruled out, or worse, people misunderstand instructions and make the problem worse. The following sections go over some of the different communication methods used for collaboration and describe what works and what doesn't in each.

Conference Calls

Conference calls are one of the most common and one of the absolute worst ways to communicate for problem solving. The biggest problem is that only one person can talk on a conference call at a time. Even if you are fortunate and only have people who are directly working an issue on the call, anyone who has new information, a breakthrough, a warning, or anything else has to wait their turn to speak. Even when they do get their turn, there's no guarantee everyone will understand what they said the first time between interruptions, bad cell signals, and background noise from speakerphone users who forgot to mute. It is especially difficult to communicate command-line commands, IP addresses, log output, or anything else that's remotely technical.

If solving a problem quickly is important, than conference calls put a number of obstacles in your way. First and foremost is the time you spend to look up the conference call number and access code, punch everything in, and then wait while the "moderator" joins the conference. Once the conference call is connected, you can expect the first five to ten minutes to be a complete wash as your conversation goes something like this:

BEEP "___ just joined the conference."

Fred: "Who just joined?"

Ted: "It's Ted. So the website is down! What do you think the problem is?"

Fred: "Well I'm not sure yet . . . I just logged into the . . ."

BEEP "Mary just joined the conference."

Mary: "Hey so the website is down? What do you think the problem is?"

Fred: "I just logged into the web server and I'm looking at the . . ."

BEEP "Bob just joined the conference."

Bob: (*highway noises in the background*) "Hey the website is down!"

The fact is, most problem-solving teams aren't alone on the conference call. Many managers love conference calls as a way to be involved in the troubleshooting process and as a central command to "manage" the issue even if they can't directly contribute. This inevitably results in frequent requests for a progress report, which means someone (likely the team lead who you most want to work the issue) stops what they are doing to explain. Since only one person can talk on the call at once, during the explanation no other member of the team can communicate.

Essentially all of the other communication methods listed below are preferable to conference calls, so while I'm not saying throw away your conference call number, I am saying you should make it your last resort.

Direct Conversation

It's common for offices to seat teams together in the same area, yet even when every team member is within earshot, often people turn to a conference call to communicate during a crisis. If everyone is within earshot there are many advantages to discussing an issue out loud. For one, it's generally easier to understand what someone says, and secondly, it's easier for multiple conversations to occur at one time.

The downside to direct conversations for problem solving is that it is still difficult to share any relatively technical information, much less long log entries or URLs. On top of that, usually conversations aren't recorded, so there's no record of your troubleshooting steps for a later postmortem, and anyone who joins the conversation late needs to be brought up to speed. Plus if everyone doesn't work in the same location, or the problem occurs after-hours, then you are back to the conference call. For me, direct conversations are a good supplement for some of the other, better communication methods.

Email

Email can be a good way to collaborate on a problem, especially if it isn't time sensitive. You can see examples of this in the public bug-tracking systems for popular open source projects. The advantages of email over voice communication are

※ Multiple conversations can occur at once.

※ Side conversations are also easy.

※ It's easy to paste in IP addresses, URLs, or commands.

※ You can attach screenshots or logs.

※ Someone who joined in the problem late can read the email thread and get up to speed by themselves.

※ You automatically have a time-stamped log of the troubleshooting collaboration process that might include pasted command output and other data that might not get logged any other way.

That said, a number of problems still exist with email communication. For one, email isn't real-time and interactive, so there is always a lag you wouldn't have when talking to someone in person, and that can really slow down the troubleshooting process. Secondly, long email chains can be difficult to parse and read, especially when people have different philosophies when it comes to top-posting versus bottom-posting versus inline replies. It's very easy to overlook critical information that might be nested between comments or pasted output. If you are an administrator and have monitoring software installed, you likely use email for one of the notifications. During an issue, your inbox might be filled with alerts, so it could be difficult to find the conversation in the middle of so many other emails. Finally, what if the problem you were trying to solve is why the email server was down?

Real-Time Chat Rooms

Real-time chat rooms are one of the best ways for a team to collaborate when troubleshooting. Real-time chat rooms include IRC or any instant messaging client such as Jabber that has a group chat feature. Here are some of the advantages chat rooms have over the other methods of communication:

- Communication is real-time and interactive.

- Multiple people can communicate at the same time.

- Individuals can also chat privately.

- It is easy to paste in technical information.

- Most chat room software includes a file-sharing feature so you can share screenshots or logs.

- Chat room conversations can be logged for later postmortems.

- Some chat rooms keep chat history even for new people who join, so it's easy to get up to speed.

- You can ignore the conversation when you are focused on something, then return to the conversation and catch up.

- You can set the chat room title to the current state of the problem and please your manager.

Chat rooms aren't without their own issues, though. For one, only some chat room software saves chat history. Without that feature, every new collaborator who joins the chat will need to be brought up to speed. Also, any pasted text that is more than a few lines long can be difficult to read in a chat room, so you might need to resort to email or some other method to share large amounts of data. Finally, some people just prefer talking over typing, especially if they aren't fast typists, so you may have a hard time getting them to join the chat room.

It may go without saying, but for the sake of privacy, it is better to use a chat server under your own control since during troubleshooting sessions a lot of sensitive data gets shared. Both IRC and Jabber offer open source servers you can install in your environment to make sure communication stays within your control.

Have a Backup Communication Method

Whatever communication method you choose, you will want to make sure you have a backup in place. It's tough to communicate over email if the email server is down, and if you have networking problems, you might not be able to reach your internal chat server. Figure out ahead of time how you will communicate in case your primary method won't work, and make sure everyone knows how to use it.

Favor Quick, Simple Tests over Slow, Complex Tests

It would be great if every problem had a logical set of tests along with an order in which you should try them. Instead, often you come up with a few different possible causes that seem equally plausible. It can be difficult to know what you should try first, but a good rule of thumb is that when you have two equally good tests to perform, favor quick or simple tests over slow or complex ones.

If you are part of an organization where downtime is measured in dollars, it's often important to locate the root cause of a problem as quickly as possible. For instance, when a web server is down, there are a number of different ways to troubleshoot the problem, but if you start by trying to ping the server, you are performing a fast test that immediately tells you whether the server is still on the network. If ping doesn't work you can start working on how to get the server back on the network. If ping does work, you can start the longer, more involved troubleshooting process, but you are only out a couple of seconds.

In a team setting you have an advantage in that it's easier to do more than one test at a time. In this case, it might make sense to have one member work on a slow, complex test while someone else focuses on shorter, simpler tests. As long as everyone communicates well, you can quickly drill down to a root cause this way.

Although quick and simple tests should be preferred, it's fine to start a slow test *if* it's mostly unattended. The reason for this is that you can fire off the slow test and then work on other things while it runs. The same thinking applies to any other troubleshooting processes that take some time. For instance, if as part of the troubleshooting process you need to file a ticket or send some sort of notice to other support staff, get that process started and then dive into other tasks that require more focus.

Here's another great question to ask: "Is it plugged in?" Often some of the largest problems have the simplest causes. Network and power cables are often loosely connected and the slightest nudge is enough to drop your server from the network. If you are close enough to a system to check whether it's plugged in, it's better to do that quick visual test than sit at your computer waiting for a minute-long port scan to return.

Favor Past Solutions

The fact of the matter is that most problems happen more than once. One of the reasons that some people have an uncanny ability to isolate an issue quickly is that they have experienced the same thing many times before. You will become a better and faster troubleshooter the more problems you are exposed to.

When you are solving a problem you will often see the same symptoms that you've seen before. Try to remember what the root cause was the last time and what steps you used to isolate the issue. More often than not, when the symptoms are the same, the root cause will be the same, and if you are able to recognize that, you can solve the problem that much faster. Like they say, if it walks like a duck and quacks like a duck, it's probably a duck.

Yet, sometimes it's not a duck. I've seen some people take the principle of favoring past solutions so far that if any symptoms sound familiar, they become completely closed off to any other explanation. The fact is, completely different problems can often have the same symptoms, especially on the surface. For instance, an ssh session into a server can lag and seem sluggish both when the server is under heavy load or when the network connection is saturated. Nmap (a useful port scanning tool) will report that a port is filtered both if a firewall is blocking it and if there is a router misconfiguration. If you zero in on a past solution too quickly, you can bias yourself and make it much more difficult to find the real problem.

The key is that even when you use past solutions to guide your trouble-shooting process, still be sure to test your hypotheses. If you remember some of the ways you isolated the issue last time, you should be able to prove it with a test much faster this time, and if your test gives different results, be ready to move on to other theories.

Document Your Problems and Solutions

As I've already mentioned, most problems happen more than once. One of the best ways to take advantage of this fact is to document your problems and their solutions. Many places call this process a postmortem. After a problem is resolved, everyone involved gets together and documents what went wrong and what steps everyone performed to isolate the issue along with their results. At the end of the postmortem a root cause is identified and, ideally, further steps are put in place to prevent the problem from happening again.

While postmortems take time out of everyone's busy schedule, there are a lot of reasons they are worth doing. The main reason is that in the event the same symptoms do creep up again, it can be hard to remember every-thing you did the last time to resolve the issue. In the heat of the moment, often all you can remember is that you've seen the issue before. If you can find a matching postmortem, you'll get an immediate list of troubleshoot-ing steps to isolate the issue.

In a team setting, this documentation process makes everyone a better problem solver. The junior members of the team get the benefit of learn-ing from more senior members' experience, and everyone learns new tools and techniques together. What's more, when the solutions to problems are documented, it's easier for junior team members to solve the problem by themselves. That means fewer wake-up calls when you aren't on call and fewer interruptions when you are on vacation.

When done properly, postmortems can be a valuable asset, but when done poorly, they can cause more problems than they solve. It's great to talk about and document troubleshooting techniques and procedures, but you must also trace back to the root cause. It's true that it takes extra time and effort to pore through logs to trace the root cause once the problem goes away. Many times a team will go only as far as it takes to describe the symptoms and what they did to make the problem go away. These are often the same teams that only solve problems by rebooting servers or services. If you don't isolate a root cause, you are probably going to see the same problem again and again.

Of course, isolating a root cause is only useful if you then take some steps to prevent the problem from happening again. Once you know the root cause, you can then figure out how to fix it and who will take it on. That is often easier said than done but, again, without it you will likely see the problem again, and worst case, you can decide that the effort involved to solve a problem for good isn't worth it.

Some teams, if you can call them that, have the opposite problem. They love to use the postmortem to isolate a root cause, but only so they know who to blame. Postmortems in this environment become defensive, often aggressive, and ultimately counterproductive. When a postmortem becomes all about blame, people are less likely to participate and more likely to keep facts to themselves, especially if they think it could implicate them. In the end, even if you do find someone to blame, you may not have found the actual root cause. This fosters an even more dysfunctional environment when you have to troubleshoot a new issue. Instead of solving the problem at hand, the focus is on doing enough to prove the problem is "on your end, not mine."

Finally, some people love postmortems so much that they start them before the problem is even solved. When you are in the middle of a crisis, your focus should be strictly on the problem at hand and the troubleshooting steps you will perform to isolate it. It's too early to know the root cause, so what good is it to say those immortal words: "What can we do so this never happens again?" If you've ever solved complex problems, you know that what you think might be the root cause can change multiple times throughout the process. Often troubleshooting environments are high-stress and require extreme focus, especially when the problem is costing your company money and any distractions just mean it will be that much longer before the problem is solved.

Even if you have just identified the root cause, it's still better to allow enough time for everyone to cool off, calm down, and really think about what just happened before you plan long-term solutions. Without that extra time, you are more likely to come up with reactionary, bandage fixes that either postpone the problem or create more problems than they solve.

Know What Changed

One of the largest sources of problems in a system is change. When everything has been running smoothly for a long time and then a problem appears, one of the first things you should ask is "What changed?" Now, if your system is constantly unstable, you wouldn't necessarily want to jump to new changes as a source of your problems; but on a stable, consistent system, all other things being equal, changes should be your first trouble-shooting target. Identifying and ruling out changes made to the system will dramatically speed up your troubleshooting process.

Although a change to the system could likely be the source of the problem, if you have no way to track changes, you will probably not be able to solve the problem any faster. If you don't have some way to keep track of changes, you should seriously consider one—especially once your system is stable. Nothing is nicer than getting an alert of a problem, having someone pipe up with "Jim pushed a code change around the time the problem started," and immediately tracking down the issue. Nothing's worse than discovering a problem on a stable system, asking what changed, and realizing that you have no way of knowing.

Even with some way to keep track of your changes, it's still best if you can discipline yourself to change only one thing at a time. It's much simpler to isolate an issue if you can point to a single change made around the time of the problem; it's much more difficult if ten different pieces of code and three configuration files were changed at the same time. I've seen some teams use maintenance windows as a way to get a lot of unrelated things knocked out at once. The issue is that when a problem arises during that maintenance window, it's much harder to isolate the root cause.

It's great if you have a system to keep track of your changes, but even better is a system that allows you to roll back any changes that cause problems. If nothing else, if you can roll back all changes to the system before the problem appeared and the problem is still there, you have just ruled out a major hypothesis and can move on to other tests. Even if you have the ability to roll back changes, still try to change one thing at a time. Rolling back a large group of changes may solve the problem, but you still have to dig through each individual change to find the source of the problem.

Having said all of this, changes aren't always the cause of your problems. In fact, I've seen the "What changed?" question create many red herrings in troubleshooting sessions. Like with all of these troubleshooting philosophies, be sure to test your change hypothesis and don't just start rolling everything back at the first sign of an issue.

Understand How Systems Work

One thing I've learned in my years as a systems administrator is that when there's a problem, everyone blames the technology they understand least. At one point in my career, DNS became the scapegoat for any and all networking problems. I have no idea how it started, since as long as I had been there our DNS servers had always been stable, but the moment any networking problem appeared heads would pop up above cubicles and people would say "Is DNS down?" What I noticed was that those people who were blaming DNS were the same people who knew the least about it. My solution was to host a voluntary class inside the company where I taught how DNS worked, and afterward I noticed that everyone who had attended the class stopped blaming DNS for networking problems (and the few people who skipped the class still did).

The point is that this instinct to blame the technology you understand least applies to you the troubleshooter as well as anyone else. You will be a much more effective problem solver if you understand how the system you are troubleshooting works. From the perspective of solving Linux issues, this means having a good understanding of TCP/IP, DNS, Linux processes, programming, and memory management. This book will help explain many of these subjects in the context of troubleshooting, but the fact is they are good subjects to know anyway even outside of troubleshooting.

You'll discover that the more you understand how a system works, the faster you will be able to solve its problems. You will find you can trust your hunches about a problem more. It also will help you avoid wild goose chases. You'll be able to rule out entire categories of root causes without having to perform many tests.

Use the Internet, but Carefully

The Internet can be a very valuable resource when troubleshooting. You probably aren't the first person in the world to see a particular error message. It's not only likely that someone else has seen the same symptoms as you, there's a good chance in your search you'll find a working solution.

The challenge with using the Internet for your troubleshooting is that you must have a good, clear understanding of the problem *before* you search on the Internet. If your server is not on the network and you type "server not on network" into a search engine, you probably won't get very helpful results. Once you do some troubleshooting steps on your own to narrow down the issue and have a clearer understanding of the problem, you'll be able to use specific, targeted search queries that very well could help you solve your problem.

I've found the Internet to be most useful when troubleshooting problems that include a very specific error code or phrase. Error codes that describe a specific issue can be handy because they are simple to search for even if you don't understand what the error code means. Usually you'll find a helpful person on a forum or knowledge base that explains what the error code means and what to do when you see it. Error messages in program output, if they are specific enough, can also be a good source for help when you are trying to resolve a problem.

The danger with Internet searches is that if you don't have a good understanding of the problem or don't use specific search queries, you can end up with a lot of bad information and bad troubleshooting steps that will take you further away from the root cause. You can also find a lot of advice from people who frankly don't know what they are talking about. Always consider the source, and especially be sure you understand any commands or code before you copy and paste them.

Resist Rebooting

Back in the Windows 95 days, rebooting was often the best way to fix just about any problem. We aren't in the Windows 95 days anymore, nor are we even using Windows here, yet some people are still stuck in that mindset, so the moment a problem arises, their first action is to restart a service or reboot hardware.

The most dangerous thing about rebooting to fix a problem isn't that it won't work, but that sometimes it actually does fix the problem. What's dangerous is that if it does fix the problem you are still no closer to identifying the root cause, and, since the problem is no longer there to test again, you may never isolate the cause. It is really difficult if not impossible to troubleshoot the cause of a problem when the problem no longer exists. If you don't isolate the root cause, you are almost guaranteeing you will see the problem again at a later date.

Don't get me wrong, I'm not saying that you should never reboot hardware or restart a service when troubleshooting. What I am saying is that you should always use a reboot as an absolute last resort, and try to capture all of the troubleshooting data you can beforehand just in case the problem does go away. This can be a tricky policy to have, especially if the problem is costing real money and your boss or a customer is screaming at you to just reboot and see if it fixes things. Stick to your guns, though. If you think your boss or customer is upset now, wait until the same problem happens again.

## CHAPTER 2

Why Is the Server So Slow? Running Out of CPU, RAM, and Disk I/O

ALTHOUGH MOST OF THE problems you'll find on a server have some basis in networking, a class of issues still involves only the localhost. What makes this tricky is that some local and networking problems often create the same set of symptoms, and in fact, local problems can create network problems and vice versa. This chapter covers problems that occur specifically on a host and leaves issues that impact the network to Chapter 5.

Just about everyone in a DevOps team faces problems with a sluggish or unresponsive host, whether they are a developer trying to track down why their latest check-in is running much slower than before, a QA engineer trying to perform load tests before their code hits production, or a sysadmin who needs to figure out whether it's time to buy more RAM, extra CPUs, or faster disks. These same techniques can even help you troubleshoot load problems on your Linux desktop.

Probably one of the most common problems you will find on a host is that it is sluggish to the point of being unresponsive. Often this can be caused by network issues, but this chapter will discuss some local troubleshooting tools you can use to tell the difference between a loaded network and a loaded machine.

When a machine is sluggish, it is often because you have consumed all of a particular resource on the system. The main resources are CPU, RAM, disk I/O, and network (which I will leave to Chapter 5). Overuse of any of these resources can cause a system to bog down to the point that often the only recourse is your last resort—a reboot. If you can log in to the system, however, there are a number of tools you can use to identify the cause.

System Load

System load average is probably the fundamental metric you start from when troubleshooting a sluggish system. One of the first commands I run when I'm troubleshooting a slow system is uptime:

```
$ uptime
13:35:03 up 103 days, 8 min, 5 users, load average: 2.03, 20.17, 15.09
```

The three numbers after load average—2.03, 20.17, and 15.09—represent the 1-, 5-, and 15-minute load averages on the machine, respectively. A system load average is equal to the average number of processes in a runnable or uninterruptible state. Runnable processes are either currently using the CPU or waiting to do so, and uninterruptible processes are waiting for I/O.

A single-CPU system with a load average of 1 means the single CPU is under constant load. If that single-CPU system has a load average of 4, there is four times the load on the system than it can handle, so three out of four processes are waiting for resources. The load average reported on a system is not tweaked based on the number of CPUs you have, so if you have a two-CPU system with a load average of 1, one of your two CPUs is loaded at all times—that is, you are 50% loaded. So a load of 1 on a single-CPU system is the same as a load of 4 on a four-CPU system in terms of the amount of available resources used.

The 1-, 5-, and 15-minute load averages describe the average amount of load over that respective period of time and are valuable when you try to determine the current state of a system. The 1-minute load average will give you a good sense of what is currently happening on a system, so in the previous example, you can see that the server most recently had a load of 2 over the last minute, but the load had spiked over the last 5 minutes to an average of 20. Over the last 15 minutes the load was an average of 15. This tells us that the machine had been under high load for at least 15 minutes and the load appeared to increase around 5 minutes ago, but it appears to have subsided. Let's compare this with a completely different load average:

```
$ uptime
05:11:52 up 20 days, 55 min, 2 users, load average: 17.29, 0.12, 0.01
```

In this case, both the 5- and 15-minute load averages are low, but the 1-minute load average is high, so I know that this spike in load is relatively recent. Often in this circumstance I will run uptime multiple times in a row (or use a tool like top, which I will discuss in a moment) to see whether the load is continuing to climb or is on its way back down.

What Is a High Load Average?

A fair question to ask is what load average you consider to be high. The short answer is "It depends on what is causing it." Because the load describes the average number of active processes that are using resources, a spike in load could mean a few things. What is important to determine is whether the load is CPU-bound (processes waiting on CPU resources), RAM-bound (specifically, high RAM usage that has moved into swap), or I/O-bound (processes fighting for disk or network I/O).

For instance, if you run an application that generates a high number of simultaneous threads at different points, and all of those threads are launched at once, you might see your load spike to 20, 40, or higher as they all compete for system resources. As they complete, the load might come right back down.

Typically systems seem to be more responsive when under CPU-bound load than when under I/O-bound load. I've seen systems with loads in the hundreds that were CPU-bound, and I could still run diagnostic tools on those systems with pretty good response times. On the other hand, I've seen systems with relatively low I/O-bound loads on which just logging in took a minute because the disk I/O was completely saturated. A system that runs out of RAM resources often appears to have I/O-bound load, since once the system starts using swap storage on the disk, it can consume disk resources and cause a downward spiral as processes slow to a halt.

Diagnose Load Problems with top

One of the first tools I turn to when I need to diagnose high load is top. When you type top on the command line and press Enter, you will see a lot of system information all at once (Figure 2-1). This data will continually update so that you see live information on the system, including how long the system has been up, the load average, how many total processes are running on the system, how much memory you have—total, used, and free—and finally a list of processes on the system and how many resources they are using. You probably won't be able to see every process that is currently running on your system with top because they wouldn't all fit on the

```
top - 15:28:40 up 16 min,  2 users,  load average: 0.00, 0.17, 0.22
Tasks:  68 total,   1 running,  67 sleeping,   0 stopped,   0 zombie
Cpu(s):  0.0%us,   1.6%sy,  0.0%ni, 98.4%id,  0.0%wa,  0.0%hi,  0.0%si,  0.0%st
Mem:   508684k total,  304116k used,  204568k free,   10976k buffers
Swap:  397304k total,       0k used,  397304k free,  138948k cached

  PID USER      PR  NI  VIRT  RES  SHR S %CPU %MEM    TIME+  COMMAND
 1331 ubuntu    20   0  2308 1124  896 R  1.6  0.2   0:00.75 top
    1 root      20   0  2616 1576 1192 S  0.0  0.3   0:01.07 init
    2 root      20   0     0    0    0 S  0.0  0.0   0:00.00 kthreadd
    3 root      RT   0     0    0    0 S  0.0  0.0   0:00.00 migration/0
    4 root      20   0     0    0    0 S  0.0  0.0   0:00.00 ksoftirqd/0
    5 root      RT   0     0    0    0 S  0.0  0.0   0:00.00 watchdog/0
    6 root      20   0     0    0    0 S  0.0  0.0   0:00.49 events/0
    7 root      20   0     0    0    0 S  0.0  0.0   0:00.00 cpuset
    8 root      20   0     0    0    0 S  0.0  0.0   0:00.00 khelper
    9 root      20   0     0    0    0 S  0.0  0.0   0:00.00 netns
   10 root      20   0     0    0    0 S  0.0  0.0   0:00.00 async/mgr
   11 root      20   0     0    0    0 S  0.0  0.0   0:00.00 pm
   12 root      20   0     0    0    0 S  0.0  0.0   0:00.02 sync_supers
   13 root      20   0     0    0    0 S  0.0  0.0   0:00.00 bdi-default
   14 root      20   0     0    0    0 S  0.0  0.0   0:00.00 kintegrityd/0
   15 root      20   0     0    0    0 S  0.0  0.0   0:00.04 kblockd/0
   16 root      20   0     0    0    0 S  0.0  0.0   0:00.00 kacpid
   17 root      20   0     0    0    0 S  0.0  0.0   0:00.00 kacpi_notify
   18 root      20   0     0    0    0 S  0.0  0.0   0:00.00 kacpi_hotplug
   19 root      20   0     0    0    0 S  0.0  0.0   0:00.00 ata/0
   20 root      20   0     0    0    0 S  0.0  0.0   0:00.00 ata_aux
   21 root      20   0     0    0    0 S  0.0  0.0   0:00.00 ksuspend_usbd
   22 root      20   0     0    0    0 S  0.0  0.0   0:00.00 khubd
```

Figure 2-1 Standard top output

screen. By default top sorts the processes according to how much CPU they use. That way you can see what processes are consuming CPU at a glance.

So what if you do notice a process consuming all of your CPU and you want to kill it? The very first column for processes in top is labeled PID and shows a program's process ID—a unique number assigned to every process on a system. To kill a process, press the K key and then type in the PID you wish to kill; then hit Enter when prompted to kill with signal 15.

By default top runs in an interactive mode, which is fine unless you want to view information that doesn't fit on the screen. If you do want to view the full output of top, or redirect it to a file, you can run it in a batch mode. The -b option enables batch mode, and the -n option lets you control how many times top will update before it closes. So, for instance, to run top just once so you can see the full output, run

```
$ top -b -n 1
```

If you wanted to store that information into a file named top_output, use

```
$ top -b -n 1 > top_output
```

If you wanted to view the top output *and* output to a file at the same time, you could use the handy command-line tool tee:

```
$ top -b -n 1 | tee top_output
```

Make Sense of top Output

When you use top to diagnose load, the basic steps are to examine the top output to identify what resources you are running out of (CPU, RAM, disk I/O). Once you have figured that out, you can try to identify what processes are consuming those resources the most. First, let's examine some standard top output from a system:

```
top - 14:08:25 up 38 days,  8:02,  1 user,  load average: 1.70, 1.77, 1.68
Tasks: 107 total,   3 running, 104 sleeping,   0 stopped,   0 zombie
Cpu(s): 11.4%us, 29.6%sy,  0.0%ni, 58.3%id,  .7%wa, 0.0%hi, 0.0%si, 0.0%st
Mem:   1024176k total,   997408k used,    26768k free,    85520k buffers
Swap: 1004052k total,     4360k used,   999692k free,   286040k cached

  PID USER      PR  NI  VIRT  RES  SHR S %CPU %MEM    TIME+  COMMAND
 9463 mysql     16   0  686m 111m 3328 S   53  5.5 569:17.64  mysqld
18749 nagios    16   0  140m 134m 1868 S   12  6.6 1345:01  nagios2db_status
24636 nagios    17   0 34660  10m  712 S    8  0.5 1195:15  nagios
22442 nagios    24   0  6048 2024 1452 S    8  0.1  0:00.04  check_time.pl
```

The first line of output is the same as you would see from the uptime command. As you can see in this case, the machine isn't too heavily loaded for a four-CPU machine:

```
top - 14:08:25 up 38 days,  8:02,  1 user,  load average: 1.70, 1.77, 1.68
```

top provides you with extra metrics beyond standard system load, though. For instance, the Cpu(s) line gives you information about what the CPUs are currently doing:

```
Cpu(s): 11.4%us,  29.6%sy,  0.0%ni,  58.3%id,  0.7%wa,  0.0%hi,  0.0%si,  0.0%st
```

These abbreviations may not mean much if you don't know what they stand for, so I've broken each of them down here:

- **us: user CPU time**

  This is the percentage of CPU time spent running users' processes that aren't niced. (**Nicing** is a process that allows you to change its priority in relation to other processes.)

- **sy: system CPU time**

  This is the percentage of CPU time spent running the kernel and kernel processes.

- **ni: nice CPU time**

  If you have user processes that have been niced, this metric will tell you the percentage of CPU time spent running them.

- **id: CPU idle time**

  This is one of the metrics that you want to be high. It represents the percentage of CPU time that is spent idle. If you have a sluggish system but this number is high, you know the cause isn't high CPU load.

- **wa: I/O wait**

  This number represents the percentage of CPU time that is spent waiting for I/O. It is a particularly valuable metric when you are tracking down the cause of a sluggish system, because if this value is low, you can pretty safely rule out disk or network I/O as the cause.

- **hi: hardware interrupts**

  This is the percentage of CPU time spent servicing hardware interrupts.

- **si: software interrupts**

  This is the percentage of CPU time spent servicing software interrupts.

- **st: steal time**

  If you are running virtual machines, this metric will tell you the percentage of CPU time that was stolen from you for other tasks.

In the previous example, you can see that the system is over 50% idle, which matches a load of 1.70 on a four-CPU system. When you diagnose a slow system, one of the first values you should look at is I/O wait so you can rule out disk I/O. If I/O wait is low, then you can look at the idle percentage. If I/O wait is high, then the next step is to diagnose what is causing high disk I/O, which I will cover momentarily. If I/O wait and idle times are low, then you will likely see a high user time percentage, so you must diagnose what is causing high user time. If the I/O wait is low and the idle percentage is high, you then know any sluggishness is not because of CPU resources, and you will have to start troubleshooting elsewhere. This might mean looking for network problems, or in the case of a web server, looking at slow queries to MySQL, for instance.

Diagnose High User Time

A common and relatively simple problem to diagnose is high load due to a high percentage of user CPU time. This is common since the services on your server are likely to take the bulk of the system load and they are user processes. If you see high user CPU time but low I/O wait times, you simply need to identify which processes on the system are consuming the most CPU. By default, top will sort all of the processes by their CPU usage:

```
  PID USER      PR  NI  VIRT  RES  SHR S %CPU %MEM     TIME+  COMMAND
 9463 mysql      16   0  686m 111m 3328 S   53  5.5  569:17.64  mysqld
18749 nagios      1   0  140m 134m 1868 S   12  6.6   1345:01  nagios2db_status
24636 nagios     17   0 34660  10m  712 S    8  0.5   1195:15  nagios
22442 nagios     24   0  6048 2024 1452 S    8  0.1   0:00.04  check_time.pl
```

In this example, the mysqld process is consuming 53% of the CPU and the nagios2db_status process is consuming 12%. Note that this is the percentage of a single CPU, so if you have a four-CPU machine, you could possibly see more than one process consuming 99% CPU.

The most common high-CPU-load situations you will see are all of the CPUs being consumed either by one or two processes or by a large number of processes. Either case is easy to identify since in the first case the top process or two will have a very high percentage of CPU and the rest will be relatively low. In that case, to solve the issue you could simply kill the process that is using the CPU (hit K and then type in the PID number for the process).

In the case of multiple processes, you might have one system doing too many things. You might, for instance, have a large number of Apache processes running on a web server along with some log parsing scripts that run from cron. All of these processes might be consuming more or less the same amount of CPU. The solution to problems like this can be trickier for the long term. As in the web server example, you do need all of those Apache processes to run, yet you might need the log parsing programs as well. In the short term, you can kill (or possibly postpone) some processes until the load comes down, but in the long term, you might need to consider increasing the resources on the machine or splitting some of the functions across more than one server.

Diagnose Out-of-Memory Issues

The next two lines in the top output provide valuable information about RAM usage. Before diagnosing specific system problems, it's important to be able to rule out memory issues.

```
Mem:    1024176k total,    997408k used,    26768k free,    85520k buffers
Swap:   1004052k total,     4360k used,   999692k free,   286040k cached
```

The first line tells us how much physical RAM is available, used, free, and buffered. The second line gives us similar information about swap usage, along with how much RAM is used by the Linux file cache. At first glance it might look as if the system is almost out of RAM since the system reports that only 26,768k is free. A number of troubleshooters are misled by the used and free lines in the output because of the Linux file cache. Once Linux loads a file into RAM, it doesn't necessarily remove it from RAM when a program is done with it. If there is RAM available, Linux will cache the file in RAM so that if a program accesses the file again, it can do so much more quickly. If the system does need RAM for active processes, it won't cache as many files. Because of the file cache, it's common for a server that has been running for a fair amount of time to report a small amount of RAM free with the remainder residing in cache.

To find out how much RAM is really being used by processes, you must subtract the file cache from the used RAM. In the example code you just looked at, out of the 997,408k RAM that is used, 286,040k is being used by the Linux file cache, so that means that only 711,368k is actually being used. In this example, the system still has plenty of available memory and is barely using any swap at all. Even if you do see some swap being used, it is not necessarily an indicator of a problem. If a process becomes idle, Linux will often page its memory to swap to free up RAM for other processes. A good way to tell whether you are running out of RAM is to look at the file cache. If your actual used memory minus the file cache is high, and the swap usage is also high, you probably do have a memory problem.

If you do find you have a memory problem, the next step is to identify which processes are consuming RAM. top sorts processes by their CPU usage by default, so you will want to change this to sort by RAM usage instead. To do this, keep top open and hit the M key on your keyboard. This will cause top to sort all of the processes on the page by their RAM usage:

```
  PID USER      PR  NI  VIRT  RES  SHR S %CPU %MEM    TIME+  COMMAND
18749 nagios    16   0  140m 134m 1868 S   12  6.6  1345:01  nagios2db_status
 9463 mysql     16   0  686m 111m 3328 S   53  5.5   569:17  mysqld
24636 nagios    17   0 34660  10m  712 S    8  0.5  1195:15  nagios
22442 nagios    24   0  6048 2024 1452 S    8  0.1  0:00.04  check_time.pl
```

Look at the %MEM column and see if the top processes are consuming a majority of the RAM. If you do find the processes that are causing high RAM usage, you can decide to kill them, or, depending on the program, you might need to perform specific troubleshooting to find out what is making that process use so much RAM.

NOTE   top can actually sort its output by any of the columns. To change which column top sorts by, hit the F key to change to a screen where you can choose the sort column. After you press a key that corresponds to a particular column (for instance, K for the CPU column), you can hit Enter to return to the main top screen.

The Linux kernel also has an out-of-memory (OOM) killer that can kick in if the system runs dangerously low on RAM. When a system is almost out of RAM, the OOM killer will start killing processes. In some cases this might be the process that is consuming all of the RAM, but this isn't guaranteed. It's possible the OOM killer could end up killing programs like sshd or other processes instead of the real culprit. In many cases, the system is unstable enough after one of these events that you find you have to reboot it to ensure that all of the system processes are running. If the OOM killer does kick in, you will see lines like the following in your /var/log/syslog:

```
1228419127.32453_1704.hostname:2,S:Out of Memory: Killed process  21389 (java).
1228419127.32453_1710.hostname:2,S:Out of Memory: Killed process  21389 (java).
```

Diagnose High I/O Wait

When you see high I/O wait, one of the first things you should check is whether the machine is using a lot of swap. Since a hard drive is much slower than RAM, when a system runs out of RAM and starts using swap, the performance of almost any machine suffers. Anything that wants to access the disk has to compete with swap for disk I/O. So first diagnose whether you are out of memory and, if so, manage the problem there. If you do have plenty of RAM, you will need to figure out which program is consuming the most I/O.

It can sometimes be difficult to figure out exactly which process is using the I/O, but if you have multiple partitions on your system, you can narrow it down by figuring out which partition most of the I/O is on. To do this, you will need the iostat program, which is provided by the sysstat package in both Red Hat- and Debian-based systems; if it isn't installed, you can install it with your package manager.

Preferably you will have this program installed before you need to diagnose an issue. Once the program is installed, you can run iostat without any arguments to see an overall glimpse of your system:

```
$ sudo iostat
Linux 2.6.24-19-server (hostname)    01/31/2009

avg-cpu:  %user   %nice %system %iowait  %steal   %idle
           5.73    0.07    2.03    0.53    0.00   91.64
```

Device:	tps	Blk_read/s	Blk_wrtn/s	Blk_read	Blk_wrtn
sda	9.82	417.96	27.53	30227262	1990625
sda1	6.55	219.10	7.12	15845129	515216
sda2	0.04	0.74	3.31	53506	239328
sda3	3.24	198.12	17.09	14328323	1236081

The first bit of output gives CPU information similar to what you would see in top. Below it are I/O stats on all of the disk devices on the system as well as their individual partitions. Here is what each of the columns represents:

✳ **tps**
This lists the transfers per second to the device. "Transfers" is another way to say I/O requests sent to the device.

✳ **Blk_read/s**
This is the number of blocks read from the device per second.

✳ **Blk_wrtn/s**
This is the number of blocks written to the device per second.

✳ **Blk_read**
In this column is the total number of blocks read from the device.

✳ **Blk_wrtn**
In this column is the total number of blocks written to the device.

When you have a system under heavy I/O load, the first step is to look at each of the partitions and identify which partition is getting the heaviest I/O load. Say, for instance, that you have a database server and the database itself is stored on /dev/sda3. If you see that the bulk of the I/O is coming from there, you have a good clue that the database is likely consuming the I/O.

Once you figure that out, the next step is to identify whether the I/O is mostly from reads or writes. Let's say you suspect that a backup job is causing the increase in I/O. Since the backup job is mostly concerned with reading files from the file system and writing them over the network to the backup server, you could possibly rule that out if you see that the bulk of the I/O is due to writes, not reads.

You will probably have to run iostat more than one time to get an accurate sense of the current I/O on your system. If you specify a number on the command line as an argument, iostat will continue to run and give you new output after that many seconds. For instance, if you wanted to see iostat output every 2 seconds, you could type sudo iostat 2. Another useful argument to iostat if you have any NFS shares is -n. When you specify -n, iostat will give you I/O statistics about all of your NFS shares.

In addition to iostat, we have a much simpler tool available in newer distributions called iotop. In effect, it is a blend of top and iostat in that it shows you all of the running processes on the system sorted by their I/O statistics. The software uses a somewhat new feature of the Linux kernel and requires the 2.6.20 kernel or later. If the program isn't installed by default, you will find it in the aptly named iotop package. It is included in Debian-based distributions, but for Red Hat-based distributions, you will need to track down and install a third-party RPM with a search on the web or via a third-party repository. Once the package is installed, you can run iotop as root and see output like the following:

```
$ sudo iotop
Total DISK READ: 189.52 K/s | Total DISK WRITE: 0.00 B/s

  TID  PRIO  USER     DISK READ  DISK WRITE  SWAPIN    IO>     COMMAND

 8169  be/4  root     189.52 K/s   0.00 B/s  0.00 %  0.00 %   rsync --server --se

 4243  be/4  kyle       0.00 B/s   3.79 K/s  0.00 %  0.00 %   cli /usr/lib/gnome-

 4244  be/4  kyle       0.00 B/s   3.79 K/s  0.00 %  0.00 %   cli /usr/lib/gnome-

    1  be/4  root       0.00 B/s   0.00 B/s  0.00 %  0.00 %   init
```

In this case, you can see that there is an rsync process tying up your read I/O.

Troubleshoot High Load after the Fact

So far this chapter has talked about how to find the cause of high load while the system is loaded. Although top and iostat are great tools, we aren't always fortunate enough to be on the system when it has problems. I can't tell you how many times I've been notified of a slow server, only to have the load drop before I log in. With only a little effort, you can install tools on your server to log performance data throughout the day.

We've already discussed how to use the tool iostat included in the sysstat package to troubleshoot high IO, but sysstat includes tools that can also report on CPU and RAM utilization. Although it's true you can already do this with top, what makes sysstat even more useful is that it provides a simple mechanism to log system statistics like CPU load, RAM, and I/O stats. With these statistics, when someone complains that a system was slow around noon yesterday, you can play back these logs and see what could have caused the problem.

Configure sysstat

The first step is to install the sysstat package using your package manager. On a Debian-based system like Ubuntu, sysstat won't be enabled automatically, so edit /etc/default/sysstat and change

ENABLED="false"

to

ENABLED="true"

On a Red Hat-based system, you may want to edit the /etc/sysconfig/sysstat file and change the HISTORY option so it logs more than 7 days of statistics. On both distributions types, statistics will be captured every 10 minutes and a daily summary will be logged.

Once enabled, sysstat gathers system stats every 10 minutes and stores them under /var/log/sysstat or /var/log/sa. In addition, it will rotate out the statistics file every night before midnight. Both of these actions are run in the /etc/cron.d/sysstat script, so if you want to change how frequently sysstat gathers information, you can modify it from that file.

View CPU Statistics

As sysstat gathers statistics, it stores them in files beginning with sa followed by the current day of the month (such as sa03). This means that you can go back up to a month from the current date and retrieve old statistics. Use the sar tool to view these statistics. By default sar outputs the CPU statistics for the current day:

```
$ sar
Linux 2.6.24-22-server (kickseed) 01/07/2012
. . .
07:44:20 PM  CPU  %user %nice %system %iowait %steal  %idle
07:45:01 PM  all  0.00  0.00   0.54    0.51    0.00   98.95
07:55:01 PM  all  0.54  0.00   1.66    1.26    0.00   96.54
08:05:01 PM  all  0.20  0.00   0.72    1.08    0.00   98.00
08:15:01 PM  all  0.49  0.00   1.12    0.62    0.00   97.77
08:25:01 PM  all  0.49  0.00   2.15    1.21    0.00   96.16
08:35:01 PM  all  0.22  0.00   0.98    0.58    0.00   98.23
08:45:01 PM  all  0.23  0.00   0.75    0.54    0.00   98.47
08:55:01 PM  all  0.20  0.00   0.78    0.50    0.00   98.52
09:01:18 PM  all  0.19  0.00   0.72    0.37    0.00   98.71
09:05:01 PM  all  0.24  0.00   1.10    0.54    0.00   98.12
Average:     all  0.32  0.00   1.12    0.78    0.00   97.78
```

From the output you can see many of the same CPU statistics you would view in top output. At the bottom, sar provides an overall average as well.

View RAM Statistics

The sysstat cron job collects much more information than CPU load, though. For instance, to gather RAM statistics instead, use the -r option:

```
$ sar -r
Linux 2.6.24-22-server (kickseed) 01/07/2012
07:44:20 PM kbmemfree kbmemused %memused kbbuffers kbcached kbswpfree kbswpused %swpused kbswpcad
07:45:01 PM   322064    193384    37.52    16056   142900    88316        0      0.00       0
07:55:01 PM   318484    196964    38.21    17152   144672    88316        0      0.00       0
08:05:01 PM   318228    197220    38.26    17648   144700    88316        0      0.00       0
08:15:01 PM   297669    217780    42.25    18384   154408    88316        0      0.00       0
08:25:01 PM   284152    231296    44.87    20072   173724    88316        0      0.00       0
08:35:01 PM   283096    232352    45.08    20612   173756    88316        0      0.00       0
08:45:01 PM   283284    232164    45.04    21116   173780    88316        0      0.00       0
08:55:01 PM   282556    232892    45.18    21624   173804    88316        0      0.00       0
09:01:18 PM   276632    238816    46.33    21964   173896    88316        0      0.00       0
09:05:01 PM   281876    233572    45.31    22188   173900    88316        0      0.00       0
Average:      294804    220644    42.81    19682   162954    88316        0      0.00       0
```

Here you can see how much free and used memory you have as well as view statistics about swap and the file cache similar to what you would see in either top or free output. The difference here is that you can go back in time.

View Disk Statistics

Another useful metric to pull from sar is disk statistics. The -b option gives you a basic list of disk I/O information:

```
$ sar -b
Linux 2.6.24-22-server (kickseed) 01/07/2012
07:44:20 PM   tps  rtps  wtps bread/s bwrtn/s
07:45:01 PM  8.03  0.00  8.03    0.00  106.61
07:55:01 PM  8.78  0.14  8.64    3.35  127.59
08:05:01 PM  7.16  0.00  7.16    0.00   61.14
08:15:01 PM  8.17  0.14  8.03    5.82  139.02
08:25:01 PM  9.50  0.06  9.44    4.09  212.62
08:35:01 PM  8.27  0.00  8.27    0.01   74.66
08:45:01 PM  8.04  0.00  8.04    0.00   71.51
08:55:01 PM  7.64  0.00  7.64    0.00   66.46
09:01:18 PM  7.11  0.00  7.11    0.36   63.73
09:05:01 PM  7.61  0.00  7.61    0.00   72.11
Average:     8.11  0.04  8.06    1.67  102.52
```

Here you can see the number of total transactions per second (tps) plus how many of those transactions were reads and writes (rtps and wtps, respectively). The bread/s column doesn't measure bread I/O, instead it tells you the average number of bytes read per second. Similarly, the bwrtn/s tells you average bytes written per second.

There are tons of individual arguments you can pass sar to pull out specific sets of data, but sometimes you just want to see everything all at once. For that, just use the -A option. That will output all of the statistics from load average, CPU load, RAM, disk I/O, network I/O, and all sorts of other interesting statistics. This can give you a good idea of what sorts of statistics sar can output, so you can then read the sar manual (type man sar) to see what flags to pass sar to see particular statistics.

View Statistics from Previous Days

Of course, so far I've just listed how to pull all of the statistics for the entire day. Often you want data from only a portion of the day. To pull out data for a certain time range, use the -s and -e arguments to specify the starting time and ending time you are interested in, respectively. For instance, if you wanted to pull CPU data just from 8:00 p.m. to 8:30 p.m., you would type

```
$ sar -s 20:00:00 -e 20:30:00
Linux 2.6.24-22-server (kickseed) 01/07/2012
08:05:01 PM CPU %user %nice %system %iowait %steal %idle
08:15:01 PM all 0.49   0.00   1.12   0.62   0.00 97.77
08:25:01 PM all 0.49   0.00   2.15   1.21   0.00 96.16
Average:    all 0.49   0.00   1.63   0.91   0.00 96.96
```

If you want to pull data from a day other than today, just use the -f option followed by the full path to the particular statistics file stored under /var/log/sysstat or /var/log/sa. For instance, to pull data from the statistics on the sixth of the month you would type

```
$ sar -f /var/log/sysstat/sa06
```

You can combine any of the other sar options as normal to pull out specific types of statistics.

## CHAPTER 3

Why Won't the System Boot? Solving Boot Problems

OF ALL THE THINGS that can go wrong with a Linux system, one of the most stressful might be a system that won't boot. After all, if you can't boot a system, it means any services it provides are completely down until you can fix it. What's more, any data you need to retrieve might depend on your ability to get the system back up and running.

It turns out that a number of different problems can prevent a system from booting. To best troubleshoot why your computer won't boot, this chapter will first describe the boot process. Once you understand the boot process, you can observe your own system and see at what point in the process it gets stuck. After describing the boot process, this chapter will highlight each major class of boot problem along with how to diagnose and fix it.

Troubleshooting boot issues is a domain traditionally for sysadmins; however, any member of a DevOps team might be responsible for keeping packages on a system up to date. When a kernel or distribution update goes badly, it's good to have all the skills you need to bring the system back up yourself.

The Linux Boot Process

Chapter 1 mentioned that if you want to be good at troubleshooting, it's important that you understand how systems work. That philosophy definitely applies to troubleshooting boot problems, especially since they can have so many different causes.

The BIOS

The very first system involved in the boot process is the BIOS (Basic Input Output System). This is the first screen you will see when you boot, and although the look varies from system to system, the BIOS initializes your hardware, including detecting hard drives, USB disks, CD-ROMs, network cards, and any other hardware it can boot from. The BIOS will then go step-by-step through each boot device based on the boot device order it is configured to follow until it finds one it can successfully boot from. In the case of a Linux server, that usually means reading the MBR (master boot record: the first 512 bytes on a hard drive) and loading and executing the boot code inside the MBR to start the boot process.

GRUB and Linux Boot Loaders

After the BIOS initializes the hardware and finds the first device to boot, the boot loader takes over. On a normal Linux server this will be the GRUB program, although in the past a different program called LILO was also used. GRUB is normally what is used when you boot from a hard drive, while systems that boot from USB, CD-ROM, or the network might use syslinux, isolinux, or pxelinux respectively as their boot loader instead of GRUB. Although the specifics of syslinux and other boot loaders are different from GRUB, they all essentially load some sort of software and read a configuration file that tells them what operating systems they can boot, where to find their respective kernels, and what settings to give the system as it boots.

When GRUB is loaded, a small bit of code (what it calls stage 1) is executed from the MBR. Since you can only fit 446 bytes of boot code into the MBR (the rest contains your partition table), GRUB's stage 1 code is just enough for it to locate the rest of the code on disk and execute that. The next stage of GRUB code allows it to access Linux file systems, and it uses that ability to read and load a configuration file that tells it what operating systems it can boot, where they are on the disk, and what options to pass them. In the case of Linux, this might include a number of different kernel versions on the disk and often includes special rescue modes that can help with troubleshooting. Usually the configuration file also describes some kind of menu you can use to see and edit all of your boot options.

On most modern systems GRUB can display a nice splash screen, sometimes with graphics and often with a countdown. Usually you will see a menu that gives you a list of operating systems you can boot from (Figure 3-1), although sometimes you have to press a key like Esc (or Shift with GRUB2) to see the menu. GRUB also allows you view and edit specific boot-time settings that can be handy during troubleshooting since you can fix mistakes that you might have made in your GRUB configuration without a rescue disk.

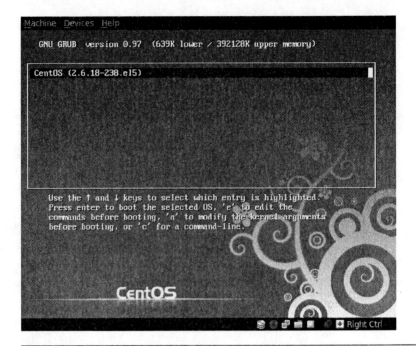

Figure 3-1 A default GRUB menu from CentOS

The Kernel and Initrd

Once you select a particular kernel in GRUB (or the countdown times out and it picks one for you), GRUB will load the Linux kernel into RAM, execute it, and pass along any boot-time arguments that were configured for it. Usually GRUB will also load an initrd (initial RAM disk) along with the kernel. This file, on a modern Linux system, is a gzipped cpio archive known as an initramfs file, and it contains a basic, small Linux root file system. On that file system are some crucial configuration files, kernel modules, and programs that the kernel needs in order to find and mount the real root file system.

In the old days all of this boot time capability would be built directly into the Linux kernel. However, as hardware support grew to include a number of different file systems and SCSI and IDE devices along with extra features like software RAID, LVM, and file system encryption, the kernel got too large. Therefore, these features were split out into individual modules so that you could load only the modules you needed for your system. Since the disk drivers and file system support were split out into modules, you were faced with a chicken or egg problem. If the modules are on the root file system, but you need those modules to read the root file system, how can you mount it? The solution was to put all those crucial modules into the initrd.

As the kernel boots, it extracts the initramfs file into RAM and then runs a script called init in the root of that initramfs. This script is just a standard shell script that does some hardware detection, creates some mount points, and then mounts the root file system. The kernel knows where the root file system is, because it was passed as one of the boot arguments (root=) by GRUB when it first loaded the kernel. The final step for the initramfs file after it mounts the real root file system is to execute the /sbin/init program, which takes over the rest of the boot process.

/sbin/init

The /sbin/init program is the parent process of every program running on the system. This process always has a PID of 1 and is responsible for starting the rest of the processes that make up a running Linux system. Those of you who have been using Linux for a while know that init on Ubuntu Server is different from what you might be used to. There are a few different standards for how to initialize a UNIX operating system, but most classic Linux distributions have used what is known as the System V init model (described momentarily), whereas some modern Linux distributions have switched to other systems like Upstart or, most recently, systemd. For instance, Ubuntu Server has switched to Upstart but has still retained most of the outward structure of System V init such as runlevels and /etc/rc?.d directories for backward compatibility; however, Upstart now manages everything under the hood. Since the most common two init systems you will run across on a server are System V init and Upstart, the following sections will describe those two.

Classic System V Init   System V refers to a particular version of the original UNIX operating system that was developed by AT&T. In this style of init, the init process reads a configuration file called /etc/inittab to discover its default runlevel, discussed next. It then enters that runlevel and starts processes that have been configured to run at that runlevel.

The System V init process is defined by different system states known as **runlevels.** Runlevels are labeled by numbers ranging from 0 to 6, and each number can potentially represent a completely different system state. For instance, runlevel 0 is reserved for a halted system state. When you enter runlevel 0, the system shuts down all running processes, unmounts all file systems, and powers off. Likewise, runlevel 6 is reserved for rebooting the machine. Runlevel 1 is reserved for **single-user mode**—a state where only a single user can log in to the system. Generally, few processes are started in single-user mode, so it is a very useful runlevel for diagnostics when a system won't fully boot. Even in the default GRUB menu you will notice a recovery mode option that boots you into runlevel 1.

Runlevels 2 through 5 are left for the distribution, and finally you, to define. The idea behind having so many runlevels is to allow you to create different modes the server could enter. Traditionally a number of Linux distributions have set one runlevel for a graphical desktop (in Red Hat, this was runlevel 5) and another runlevel for a system with no graphics (Red Hat used runlevel 3 for this). You could define other runlevels too— for instance, one that starts up a system without network access. Then when you boot, you could pass an argument at the boot prompt to override the default runlevel with the runlevel of your choice. Once the system is booted, you can also change the current runlevel with the init command followed by the runlevel. So, to change to single-user mode, you might type sudo init 1.

In addition to /etc/inittab, a number of other important files and directories for a System V init system organize start-up and shutdown scripts, or init scripts, for all of the major services on the system:

※ **/etc/init.d**
   This directory contains all of the start-up scripts for every service at every runlevel. Typically these are standard shell scripts, and they conform to a basic standard. Each script accepts at least two arguments, start and stop, which respectively start up or stop a service (such as,

say, your web server). In addition, init scripts commonly accept a few extra options such as restart (stops and then starts the service), status (returns the current state of a service), reload (tells the service to reload its settings from its configuration files), and force-reload (forces the service to reload its settings). When you run an init script with no arguments, it should generally return a list of arguments that it accepts.

/etc/rc0.d through /etc/rc6.d
These directories contain the init scripts for each respective runlevel. In practice, these are generally symlinks into the actual files under /etc/ init.d. What you will notice, however, is that the init scripts in these directories have special names assigned to them that start with an *S* (start), *K* (kill), or *D* (disable) and then a number. When init enters a runlevel, it runs every script that begins with a *K* in numerical order and passes the stop argument, but only if the corresponding init script was started in the previous runlevel. Then init runs every script that begins with an *S* in numerical order and passes the start argument. Any scripts that start with *D* init ignores—this allows you to temporarily disable a script in a particular runlevel, or you could just remove the symlink altogether. So if you have two scripts, S01foo and S05bar, init would first run S01foo start and then S05bar start when it entered that particular runlevel.

/etc/rcS.d
In this directory you will find all of the system init scripts that init runs at start-up before it changes to a particular runlevel. Be careful when you tinker with scripts in this directory because if they stall, they could prevent you from even entering single-user mode.

/etc/rc.local
Not every distribution uses rc.local, but traditionally this is a shell script set aside for the user to edit. It's generally executed at the end of the init process, so you can put extra scripts in here that you want to run without having to create your own init script.

Here is an example boot process for a standard System V init system. First init starts and reads /etc/inittab to determine its default runlevel, which in this example is runlevel 2. Then init goes to /etc/rcS.d and runs each script that begins with an S in numerical order with start as an argument. Then init does the same for the /etc/rc2.d directory. Finally init is finished but stays running in the background, waiting for the runlevel to change.

Upstart System V init is a good system and has worked well on Linux for years; however, it is not without some drawbacks. For one, init scripts don't automatically have a mechanism to respawn if the service dies. So, for instance, if the cron daemon crashes for some reason, you would have to create some other tool to monitor and restart that process.

Another issue with init scripts is that they are generally affected only by changes in runlevel or when the system starts up but otherwise are not executed unless you do so manually. Init scripts that depend on a network connection are a good example. On Red Hat and Debian-based systems an init script, called network or networking, respectively, establishes the network connection. Any init scripts that depend on a network connection are named with a higher number than this init script to ensure they run after the network script has run. What if you unplug the network cable from a server and then start it up? Well, the networking script would run, but all of the init scripts that need a network connection would time out one by one. Eventually you would get a login prompt and be able to log in. Now after you logged in, if you plugged in the network cable and restarted the networking service, you would be on the network, yet none of the services that need a network connection would automatically restart. You would have to start them manually one by one.

Upstart was designed not only to address some of the shortcomings of the System V init process, but also to provide a more robust system for managing services. One main feature of Upstart is that it is event-driven. Upstart constantly monitors the system for certain events to occur, and when they do, Upstart can be configured to take action based on those events. Some sample events might be system start-up, system shutdown, the Ctrl-Alt-Del sequence being pressed, the runlevel changing, or an Upstart script starting or stopping. To see how an event-driven system can improve on traditional init scripts, let's take the previous example of a system booted with an unplugged network cable. You could create an Upstart script that is triggered when a network cable is plugged in. That script could then restart the networking service for you. You could then configure any services that require a network connection to be triggered whenever the networking service starts successfully. Now when the system boots, you could just plug in the network cable and Upstart scripts would take care of the rest.

Upstart does not yet completely replace System V init, at least when it comes to services on the system. At the moment, Upstart does replace the functionality of init and the /etc/inittab file, and it manages changes to runlevels, system start-up and shutdown, and console ttys. More and more core functionality is being ported to Upstart scripts, but you will still find some of the standard init scripts in /etc/init.d and all of the standard symlinks in /etc/rc?.d. The difference is that Upstart now starts and stops services when runlevels change.

Upstart scripts reside in /etc/init and have different syntax from init scripts since they aren't actually shell scripts. To help illustrate the syntax, here's an example Upstart script (/etc/init/rc.conf) used to change between runlevels:

```
# rc - System V runlevel compatibility
#
# This task runs the old System V-style rc script when changing
# between runlevels.

description    "System V runlevel compatibility"
author         "Scott James Remnant <scott@netsplit.com>"
start on runlevel [0123456]
stop on runlevel [!$RUNLEVEL]
export RUNLEVEL
export PREVLEVEL
task
exec /etc/init.d/rc $RUNLEVEL
```

Upstart treats lines that begin with # as comments, like most other scripts and configuration files. The first two configuration options are start on and stop on. These lines define what events must occur for the script to start and stop. In this case, the script will start when any runlevel is entered and will stop when the runlevel is not set.

The next couple of lines export some environment variables, and then the task option tells init that this script will not be persistent—it will execute and then stop.

The actual programs that are run from an Upstart script are defined with either the script or exec options. In the case of the exec option, Upstart executes the command and all of the arguments that follow the exec option and keeps track of its PID. With the script option, Upstart treats the lines that follow as a shell script until it reaches the end script line.

Even though Upstart is designed to be event-driven, it still provides methods to check the status of Upstart jobs and start and stop them as appropriate. You can check the status, start, and stop Upstart scripts with the appropriately named status, start, and stop commands. One Upstart job on an Ubuntu server is the tty1 job and it starts the getty program on tty1. This gives an administrator a console when he or she presses Alt-F1. Let's say, however, that for some reason you believe that the console was hung. Here's how to check the status and then restart the job:

```
$ sudo status tty1
tty1: start/running, process 789
$ sudo stop tty1
tty1 stop/waiting
$ sudo start tty1
tty1 start/running, process 2251
```

You can also query the status of all available Upstart jobs with initctl list:

```
$ sudo initctl list
mountall-net stop/waiting
rc stop/waiting
rsyslog start/running, process 640
tty4 start/running, process 708
udev start/running, process 299
upstart-udev-bridge start/running, process 297
ureadahead-other stop/waiting
```

```
apport start/running
hwclock-save stop/waiting
irqbalance stop/waiting
plymouth-log stop/waiting
tty5 start/running, process 713
atd start/running, process 727
failsafe-x stop/waiting
plymouth stop/waiting
ssh start/running, process 1210
control-alt-delete stop/waiting
hwclock stop/waiting
module-init-tools stop/waiting
cron start/running, process 728
mountall stop/waiting
rcS stop/waiting
ufw start/running
mounted-varrun stop/waiting
rc-sysinit stop/waiting
tty2 start/running, process 717
udevtrigger stop/waiting
mounted-dev stop/waiting
tty3 start/running, process 718
udev-finish stop/waiting
hostname stop/waiting
mountall-reboot stop/waiting
mountall-shell stop/waiting
mounted-tmp stop/waiting
network-interface (lo) start/running
network-interface (eth0) start/running
plymouth-splash stop/waiting
tty1 start/running, process 2251
udevmonitor stop/waiting
dmesg stop/waiting
network-interface-security start/running
networking stop/waiting
procps stop/waiting
tty6 start/running, process 720
ureadahead stop/waiting
```

BIOS Boot Order

If your system can't even get to the GRUB prompt (but could previously), then either GRUB was completely removed from your MBR, your hard drive has crashed beyond recognition, or the boot order in your BIOS has changed. We'll start with how to fix the boot order since it is the simplest and fastest fix. Often this can occur when someone tweaks the BIOS boot order so they can boot off of some other media, such as a USB key, a CD-ROM, or over the network, and then they forget to change things back when they are done.

The BIOS provides a method to change its settings as the system powers on—by hitting a special key on the keyboard. Many BIOSes also allow you to press a different key and choose what device to boot from. Unfortunately, manufacturers can't seem to agree on which keys you should press to get to either option, but fortunately most BIOSes will display the keys they use on your monitor as the system powers on. Of course the emphasis is on fast boot times, so many BIOSes flash past this screen quickly. If you are lucky, your BIOS will show a quick notice on the screen (often around the time your monitor actually starts showing something) that prompts you to press a key (often Del, F1, F2, or Esc) to configure the BIOS. You might also get a prompt to press a different key (often F11 or F12) to change the BIOS boot order or to select the boot device just for this boot.

Since we want to rule out whether the BIOS boot order is the cause of our problems, if your BIOS allows you to choose the boot order on the fly, choose that option first. Otherwise, press the key to configure your BIOS and go to the screen that allows you to edit your boot order (often labeled Boot, or if not, you'll find it under Advanced). Each manufacturer's BIOS is a bit different, so you may have to look around a bit to find the right options.

Whether you select a one-time boot device or are in the BIOS config, you should be presented with a list of possible devices you can boot from. On most servers this will be some sort of hard disk, so find the first hard disk option and select it. If that drive boots properly you've found the right drive, otherwise reset the system and try each of the boot devices until you find the one that does work. If you are able to find a drive that does boot, don't forget to go back to your BIOS configuration screen and confirm that the boot order puts that drive before others.

If you don't get a GRUB prompt with any of the drives, then either GRUB is completely erased or your primary disk or disk controller has failed. First go through the steps in the next section to try to repair GRUB since they will help you use a rescue disk to determine whether the disk is available at all. If the disk isn't available at all, you'll want to turn to Chapter 10 which talks about resolving hardware failures.

Fix GRUB

The difficulty in identifying and fixing problems with GRUB is in the fact that without a functioning boot loader, you can't boot into your system and use the tools you would need to repair GRUB. There are a few different ways that GRUB might be broken on your system, but before we discuss those, you should understand that in the interest of booting quickly, some systems set GRUB with a short timeout of only a few seconds before they boot the default OS, even on servers. What's worse, some systems even hide the initial GRUB prompt from the user, so you have to press a special key (Esc for GRUB 1 releases, also known as GRUB legacy, and Shift for GRUB 2, also just known as GRUB) within a second or two after your BIOS has passed off control to GRUB.

If you don't know which version of GRUB you have installed, you may have to boot the system a few times and try out both Esc and Shift to see if you can get some sort of GRUB window to display. After that, you might still have to deal with a short timeout before GRUB boots the default OS, so you'll need to press a key (arrow keys are generally safe) to disable the timeout. The following sections discuss a few of the ways GRUB might be broken and then follow up with some general approaches to repair it.

No GRUB Prompt

The first way GRUB might be broken on your system is that it could have been completely removed from your MBR. Unfortunately, since GRUB is often hidden from the user even when it works correctly, you may not be able to tell whether GRUB is configured wrong or not installed at all. Test by pressing either the Esc or Shift keys during the boot process to confirm that no GRUB prompt appears.

It's rather rare for GRUB to disappear from the MBR completely, but it most often happens on dual-boot systems where you might load both Linux and Windows. The Windows install process has long been known to wipe out the boot code in the MBR, in which case you would get no GRUB prompt at all and instead would boot directly into Windows. Dual-boot setups are fairly rare on servers, however, so most likely if GRUB was completely removed from your MBR, your only clue would be some error from the BIOS stating that it couldn't find a suitable boot device. If you have already gone through the steps listed earlier to test your boot device order in your BIOS and still get this error, somehow GRUB was erased from the MBR.

This error might also occur on systems using Linux software RAID where the primary disk may have died. While some modern installs of GRUB can automatically install themselves to the MBR on all disks involved in a RAID, if your install doesn't default to that mode (or you are using an old version of GRUB and didn't manually install GRUB to the MBR of the other disks in your RAID array), when the primary disk dies there will be no other instance of GRUB on the remaining disks you can use.

Stage 1.5 GRUB Prompt

Another way GRUB can fail is that it can still be installed in the MBR, however, for some reason it can't locate the rest of the code it needs to boot the system. Remember that GRUB's first stage has to fit in only 446 bytes inside the MBR, so it contains the code it needs to locate and load the rest of the GRUB environment. GRUB normally loads what it calls stage 1.5 (GRUB 2 calls this core.img), which contains the code that can read Linux file systems and access the final GRUB stage, stage 2. Once stage 2 or core.img is loaded, GRUB can read its default configuration file from the file system, load any extra modules it needs, and display the normal GRUB menu. When GRUB can't find the file system that contains stage 2 or its configuration files, you might be left with a message that reads "loading stage 1.5" followed by either by an error or a simple grub> prompt.

If you get an error that loading stage 1.5 failed, move on to the section that talks about how to repair GRUB. If you get as far as a grub> prompt, that means that at least stage 1.5 did load, but it might be having trouble either loading stage 2 or reading your GRUB configuration file. This can happen if the GRUB configuration file or the stage 2 file gets corrupted, or if the file system that contains those files gets corrupted (in which case you'll want to read Chapter 4 on how to repair file systems). If you are particularly savvy with GRUB commands, or don't have access to a rescue disk, it might be possible to boot your system from the basic grub> prompt by typing the same GRUB boot commands that would be configured in your GRUB configuration file. In fact, if GRUB gets as far as the final stage and displays a prompt, you can use GRUB commands to attempt to read partitions and do some basic troubleshooting. That said, most of the time it's just simpler and faster to boot into a rescue disk and repair GRUB from there.

Misconfigured GRUB Prompt

Finally, you might find that you have a full GRUB menu loaded, but when you attempt to boot the default boot entry, GRUB fails and either returns you to the boot menu or displays an error. This usually means there are errors in your GRUB configuration file and either the disk or partition that is referenced in the file has changed (or the UUID changed, more on that in the upcoming section on how to fix a system that can't mount its root file system). If you get to this point and have an alternative older kernel or a rescue mode configured in your GRUB menu, try those and see if you can boot to the system with an older config. If so, you can follow the steps in the next section to repair GRUB from the system itself. Otherwise, if you are familiar with GRUB configuration, you can press E and attempt to tinker with the GRUB configuration from the GRUB prompt, or you can boot to a rescue disk.

Repair GRUB from the Live System

If you are fortunate enough to be able to boot into your live system (possibly with an older kernel or by tinkering with GRUB options), then you might have an easier time repairing GRUB. If you can boot into your system, GRUB was probably able to at least get to stage 2 and possibly even read its configuration file, so it's clearly installed in the MBR; the next section will go over the steps to reinstall GRUB to the MBR.

Once you are booted into the system, if the problem was with your GRUB configuration file, you can simply open up the configuration file (/boot/grub/menu.lst for GRUB 1, or /etc/default/grub for GRUB 2). In the case of GRUB 2, the real configuration file is in /boot/grub/grub.cfg, but that file is usually generated by a script and isn't intended to be edited by regular users, so once you edit /etc/default/grub, you will need to run the /usr/sbin/update-grub script to generate the new grub.cfg file. Even in the case of GRUB 1, the menu.lst file might be automatically generated by a script like update-grub depending on your distribution. If so, the distribution will usually say as much in a comment at the top of the file along with providing instructions on how to edit and update the configuration file.

Repair GRUB with a Rescue Disk

Most of the time when you have a problem with GRUB, it prevents you from booting into the system to repair it, so the quickest way to repair it is with a rescue disk. Most distributions make the process simpler for you by including a rescue disk as part of the install disk either on CD-ROM or a USB image. For instance, on a Red Hat or CentOS install disk you can type linux rescue at the boot prompt to enter the rescue mode. On an Ubuntu install disk, the rescue mode is listed as one of the options in the boot menu. For either rescue disk you should read the official documentation to find out all of the features of the rescue environment, but we will now discuss the basic steps to restore GRUB using either disk.

In the case of the Ubuntu rescue disk, after the disk boots it will present you with an option to reinstall the GRUB boot loader. You would select this option if you got no GRUB prompt at all when the system booted. Otherwise, if you suspect you just need to regenerate your GRUB configuration file, select the option to open a shell in the root environment, run update-grub to rebuild the configuration file, type exit to leave the shell, and then reboot the system.

In the case of the Red Hat or CentOS rescue disk, boot with the linux rescue boot option, then type chroot /mnt/sysimage to mount the root partition. Once the root partition is mounted and you have a shell prompt, if you need to re-install GRUB to the MBR, type /sbin/grub-install /dev/sda. Replace /dev/sda with your root partition device (if you are unsure what the device is, type df at this prompt and look to see what device it claims /mnt/sysimage is). From this prompt you can also view the /boot/grub/grub.conf file in case you need to make any custom changes to the options there.

Disable Splash Screens

Back in the earlier days of Linux, the boot process was a bit more exposed to the average user. When you booted a server, screens full of text scrolled by telling you exactly what the system was doing at any particular moment. Even on server installs, many systems default to hiding a lot of that valuable debug information.

If you've gotten past the GRUB prompt but the system gives errors further along in the boot process, you will want to disable any splash screen or other mode that suppresses output so you can see any errors. To do this, go to the GRUB menu that displays your different boot options (you may have to hit Esc or Shift at boot to display this menu), then press E to edit the boot arguments for that specific menu entry. Look for the line that contains all of your kernel boot arguments (it might start with the word linux or kernel) and edit it to remove arguments like quiet and splash. Optionally, you may add the word nosplash to make sure any splash screens are disabled. Now once you exit the editing mode and boot with these new options, you should be able to see debug output as your system boots.

Can't Mount the Root File System

Apart from GRUB errors, one of the most common boot problems is from not being able to mount the root file system. After GRUB loads the kernel and initrd file into RAM, the initrd file is expanded into an initramfs temporary root file system in RAM. This file system contains kernel modules and programs the kernel needs to locate and mount the root file system and continue the boot process. To best troubleshoot any problems in which the kernel can't mount the root file system, it's important to understand how the kernel knows where the root file system is to begin with.

The Root Kernel Argument

The kernel knows where the root file system is because of the root option passed to it by GRUB. If you were to look in a GRUB configuration file for the line that contains kernel arguments, you might see something like root=/dev/sda2, root=LABEL=/, or root=UUID=528c6527-24bf-42d1-b908-c175f7b06a0f. In the first example, the kernel is given an explicit disk partition, /dev/sda2. This method of specifying the root device is most common in older systems and has been replaced with either disk labels or UUIDs, because any time a disk is added or repartitioned, it's possible that what was once /dev/sda2 is now /dev/sdb2 or /dev/sda3.

To get around the problem of device names changing around, distributions started labeling partitions with their mount point, so the root partition might be labeled / or root and the /home partition might be labeled home or /home. Then, instead of specifying the device at the root= line, in GRUB you would specify the device label such as root=LABEL=/. That way, if the actual device names changed around, the labels would still remain the same and the kernel would be able to find the root partition.

Labels seemed to solve the problem of device names changing but introduced a different problem—what happens when two partitions are labeled the same? What started happening is that someone would add a second disk to a server that used to be in a different system. This new disk might have its own / or /home label already, and when added to the new system, the kernel might not end up mounting the labels you thought it should. To get around this issue, some distributions started assigning partitions UUIDs (Universal Unique Identifiers). The UUIDs are long strings of characters that are guaranteed to be unique across all disk partitions in the world, so you could add any disk to your system and feel confident that you will never have the same UUID twice. Now instead of specifying a disk label at the boot prompt, you would specify a UUID like root=UUID=528c6527-24bf-42d1-b908-c175f7b06a0f.

The Root Device Changed

One of the most common reasons a kernel can't mount the root partition is because the root partition it was given has changed. When this happens you might get an error along the lines of "ALERT! /dev/sdb2 does not exist" and you might then get dropped to a basic initramfs shell. On systems that don't use UUIDs, this is most often because a new disk was added and the device names have switched around (so, for instance, your old root partition was on /dev/sda2 and now it's on /dev/sdb2). If you know that you have added a disk to the system recently, go to the GRUB menu and press E to edit the boot arguments.

If you notice that you set the root argument to be a disk device, experiment with changing the device letter. So, for instance, if you have root=/dev/sda2, change it to root=/dev/sdb2 or root=/dev/sdc2. If you aren't sure how your disk devices have been assigned, you might need to boot into a rescue disk and then look through the output of a command like fdisk -l as the root user to see all of the available partitions on the system. Here's some example output of fdisk -l that shows two disks, /dev/sda and /dev/sdb. The /dev/sda disk has three partitions: /dev/sda1, /dev/sda2, and /dev/sda3, and /dev/sdb has only one: /dev/sdb1.

```
# fdisk -l

Disk /dev/sda: 11.6 GB, 11560550400 bytes
4 heads, 32 sectors/track, 176400 cylinders
Units = cylinders of 128 * 512 = 65536 bytes
Sector size (logical/physical): 512 bytes / 512 bytes
I/O size (minimum/optimal): 512 bytes / 512 bytes
Disk identifier: 0x0009c896

   Device Boot      Start         End      Blocks   Id  System
/dev/sda1               1       76279     4881840   83  Linux
/dev/sda2           76280       91904     1000000   82  Linux swap / Solaris
/dev/sda3           91905      168198     4882816   83  Linux

Disk /dev/sdb: 52.4 GB, 52429848576 bytes
4 heads, 32 sectors/track, 800016 cylinders
Units = cylinders of 128 * 512 = 65536 bytes
Sector size (logical/physical): 512 bytes / 512 bytes
I/O size (minimum/optimal): 512 bytes / 512 bytes
Disk identifier: 0x000c406f

   Device Boot      Start         End      Blocks   Id  System
/dev/sdb1               1      762924    48827120   83  Linux
```

If you find that the system does boot correctly once you change to a different device, then you can edit your GRUB configuration file (/boot/grub/grub.conf or /boot/grub/menu.lst for GRUB 1; most GRUB 2 systems use UUIDs and auto-detect the root partition) and change the root= line permanently. By the way, if the device did change, you will probably need to change the same entry in /etc/fstab as well.

For systems that use partitions labels, the inability to mount the root file system might be caused either by a disk being added that has a partition with the same label, or it could be from an administrator who changed the root partition label. The best way to diagnose disk label problems is to edit the root= line and, instead of a label, specify the disk device itself. Again, if you don't know how your disks are laid out, boot into a rescue disk and type fdisk -l. If you do find that you are able to successfully boot once you set root to a disk device instead of a label, you can either update your GRUB configuration file to use the disk device instead of a label, or you can use the program e2label to change the partition label of your root partition back to what it should be. So, for instance, to assign a label of / to /dev/sda2 as root, you would type

```
e2label /dev/sda2 /
```

In the case of duplicate labels, use the e2label tool as well to rename the duplicate root partition to be something else. You can type e2label along with just the disk device name (like e2label /dev/sda2) to display what the current label is set to.

If your system uses UUIDs and the kernel can't find the root partition, it's possible that the UUID changed. Normally the UUID should be assigned when a partition is formatted, so it is unusual for this to happen to a root partition. That said, it often happens when someone clones a system based off one that uses UUIDs. When they create the root partition for the cloned system, it gets a new UUID, yet when they copy over the GRUB configuration files, it specifies the old UUID.

Like with disk label problems, a quick way to troubleshoot this issue is to edit the boot prompt at the GRUB menu and change the root= line to specify a specific device instead of a UUID. If you find you get further along in the boot process that way, then you can use the blkid command to see the UUID that's assigned to a particular device:

```
$ sudo blkid -s UUID /dev/sda2
/dev/sda2: UUID="528c6527-24bf-42d1-b908-c175f7b06a0f"
```

Once you know what the UUID should be, you can then edit your GRUB configuration file (and /etc/fstab) so that it references the proper UUID.

The Root Partition Is Corrupt or Failed

The other main reason why a kernel may not be able to mount the root file system is that it is corrupt or the disk itself has completely failed. When a file system gets mounted, if errors are detected on the file system, it will automatically start a repair process; however, in many cases the corruption is significant enough that the boot process will drop you to a basic shell so you can manually attempt to repair the file system. If your boot process gets to this state, go to the Repair Corrupted File Systems section of Chapter 4 for details on how to correct the errors. If you fear that your disk has completely failed, check out Chapter 10, which talks about how to diagnose hardware issues.

Can't Mount Secondary File Systems

Many servers have multiple file systems that might get mounted automatically as the system boots. These file systems are defined in the /etc/fstab file and might look somewhat like the following:

```
# /etc/fstab: static file system information.
# <file system>        <mount point>    <type>  <options>        <dump>  <pass>
proc                   /proc            proc    defaults         0       0
/dev/sda1              /                ext3    defaults         0       0
/dev/sda2              swap             swap    defaults         0       0
/dev/sda3              /var             ext3    defaults         0       0
/dev/sdb1              /home            ext3    defaults         0       0
```

In this example you can see that in addition to the / partition that's on /dev/sda1, the system also mounts /var from /dev/sda3 and /home from /dev/sdb1. If either /var or /home are corrupted and can't automatically be repaired or can't be found, the boot process will stop and drop you to a shell prompt where you can investigate matters further. In these circumstances, just repeat the same troubleshooting steps you might perform for a problem with a root file system and look for device names that have changed, new labels, or different UUIDs.

Why Can't I Write to the Disk? Solving Full or Corrupt Disk Issues

4

IF YOU WERE TO ask a DevOps team to describe what part of a Linux server was the source of the most trouble for them, many would point to the hard drive. Not only is the hardware most likely to fail on your server (which we'll cover in Chapter 10), it is often also one of the main bottlenecks for your application. On top of that, if you are in charge of maintaining the server, you also have to deal with disks filling up and file systems getting corrupted. All of the latter problems start with the same symptom: A user or program can't write data to the disk.

In a DevOps organization, logging debug data is particularly valuable when you are troubleshooting your code. When one of your automated tests fails, you want to know exactly what caused the failure. All those logs add up, though, and if left to themselves they will eventually fill up the disk. When that happens, you may not automatically know which directory is using up all that space, and when processes can't write to disk, they sometimes fail in unusual ways. This chapter covers how to diagnose and fix some of the common problems that can prevent you from writing to the disk.

When the Disk Is Full

Linux actually makes it pretty obvious when you run out of disk space:

```
$ cp /var/log/syslog syslogbackup
cp: writing `syslogbackup': No space left on device
```

Of course, depending on how your system is partitioned, you may not know which partition filled up. The first step is to use the df tool to list all of your mounted partitions along with their size, used space, and available space. If you add the -h option, it shows you data in human-readable format, instead of in 1K blocks:

```
$ df -h
Filesystem      Size  Used Avail Use% Mounted on
/dev/sda1       7.8G  7.4G   60K 100% /
none            245M  192K  245M   1% /dev
none            249M     0  249M   0% /dev/shm
none            249M   36K  249M   1% /var/run
```

```
none                 249M   0  249M   0% /var/lock
none                 249M   0  249M   0% /lib/init/rw
```

Here you can see there is only one mounted partition, /dev/sda1; it has 7.8Gb of total space of which 7.4Gb is used, and it says it's 100% full with 60Kb available. Of course, with a full file system, how are you supposed to log in and fix anything? As you'll see later in the chapter, one of the common ways to free up space on a file system is to compress uncompressed logs, but if the disk has no free space, how are you expected to do that?

Reserved Blocks

If you look at the df numbers closely, though, you may say, wait a minute, is Linux really that bad at math? 7.4Gb divided by 7.8Gb is closer to 95% full.

What's happening here is that Linux has set aside a number of blocks on the file system, known as **reserved blocks,** for just such an emergency (and also to help avoid fragmentation). Only the root user can write to those reserved blocks, so if the file system gets full, the root user still has some space left on the file system to log in and move around some files. On most servers with ext-based file systems, 5% of the total blocks are reserved, but this is something you can check with the tune2fs tool if you have root permissions. For instance, here is how you would check the reserved block count on your full /dev/sda1 partition:

```
$ sudo tune2fs -l /dev/sda1 | grep -i "block count"
Block count:              2073344
Reserved block count:     103667
```

If you divide 103667 by 2073344, you'll see that it works out to about 5%, or, in this case, it means the root user has about 400Mb to play around with to try to fix the problem.

Track Down the Largest Directories

The df command lets you know how much space is used by each file system, but after you know that, you still need to figure out what is consuming all of that disk space. The similarly named du command is invaluable for this purpose. This command, with the right arguments, can scan through a file system and report how much disk space is consumed by each directory. If you pipe it to a sort command, you can then easily see which directories consume the most disk space. What I like to do is save the results in /tmp (if there's enough free space, that is) so I can refer to the output multiple times and not have to rerun du. I affectionately call this the "duck command":

```
$ cd /
$ sudo du -ckx | sort -n > /tmp/duck-root
```

This command won't output anything to the screen but instead it creates a sorted list of which directories consume the most space and outputs the list to /tmp/duck-root. If you then use tail on that file, you can see the top ten directories that use space:

```
$ sudo tail /tmp/duck-root
67872 /lib/modules/2.6.24-19-server
67876 /lib/modules
69092 /var/cache/apt
69448 /var/cache
76924 /usr/share
82832 /lib
124164 /usr
404168 /
404168 total
```

In this case, you can see that /usr takes up the most space, followed by /lib, /usr/share, and then /var/cache. Note that the output separates out /var/cache/apt and /var/cache, so you can tell that /var/cache/apt is the subdirectory that consumes the most space under /var/cache. Of course, you might have to open the duck-root file with a tool like less or a text editor so that you can see more than the last ten directories.

So what can you do with this output? In some cases the directory that takes up the most space can't be touched (as with /usr), but often when the free space disappears quickly, it is because of log files growing out of control. If you do see /var/log consuming a large percentage of your disk, you could then go to the directory and type sudo ls -lS to list all of the files sorted by their size. At that point, you could truncate (basically erase the contents of) a particular file:

```
$ sudo sh -c "> /var/log/messages"
```

Alternatively, if one of the large files has already been rotated (it ends in something like .1 or .2), you could either gzip it if it isn't already gzipped, or you could simply delete it if you don't need the log anymore. If you routinely find you have disk space problems due to uncompressed logs, you can tweak your logrotate settings in /etc/logrotate.conf and /etc/logrotate.d/ and make sure it automatically compresses rotated logs for you.

NOTE I can't count how many times I've been alerted about a full / file system (a dangerous situation that can often cause the system to freeze up) only to find out that it was caused by large files in /tmp. Specifically, these were large .swp files. When vim opens a file, it copies the entire contents into a .swp file. Certain versions of vim store this .swp file in /tmp, others in /var/tmp, and still others in ~/tmp. In any case, what had happened was that a particular user on the system decided to view an Apache log file that was gigabytes in size. When the user opened the file, it created a multi-gigabyte .swp file in /tmp and filled up the root file system. To solve the issue, I had to locate and kill the offending vim process.

Out of Inodes

Another less common but tricky situation in which you might find yourself is the case of a file system that claims it is full, yet when you run df, you see that there is more than enough space. If this ever happens to you, the first thing you should check is whether you have run out of **inodes** (an inode is a data structure that holds information about a file). When you format a file system, the mkfs tool decides at that point the maximum number of inodes to use as a function of the size of the partition.

Each new file that is created on that file system gets its own unique inode, and once you run out of inodes, no new files can be created. Generally speaking, you never get close to that maximum; however, certain servers store millions of files on a particular file system, and in those cases you might hit the upper limit. The df -i command will give you information on your inode usage:

```
$ df -i
Filesystem Inodes IUsed IFree IUse% Mounted on
/dev/sda 520192 17539 502653 4% /
```

In this example, the root partition has 520,192 total inodes but only 17,539 are used. That means you can create another 502,653 files on that file system. In the case where 100% of your inodes are used, only a few options are at your disposal. You can try to identify a large number of files that you can delete or move to another file system; you can possibly archive a group of files into a tar archive; or you can back up the files on your current file system, reformat it with more inodes, and copy the files back.

The File System Is Read-Only

Every now and then you may encounter a file system that isn't full, but it won't let you write to it all the same. When you do try to copy a file or save a file, you get an error that the file system is read-only. The first step is to see if you can, in fact, remount the file system read-write; so for instance, if the /home partition were read-only, you would type

```
$ sudo mount -o remount,rw /home
```

Chances are, though, if you get this error, it's because your file system has encountered some sort of error and has decided to remount read-only to protect itself from further damage. This sort of problem happens more frequently on virtual machines in part, I imagine, to the extra level of abstraction between its virtual disk and the physical hardware. When there's some hiccup between the two, the file system detects a serious error and protects itself. To know for sure, examine the output of the dmesg command, specifically for lines that begin with EXT3-fs error. You should see lines in the output that reference the errors ext3 found and a log entry that states Remounting filesystem read-only.

So what do you do if this happens to you? If the file system is not the root partition and you can completely unmount it, you can try to unmount it completely and then remount it. If it's the root partition, or remounting doesn't work, unfortunately you will have to reboot the system so it can check and remount the file system cleanly. If after a reboot the file system still won't mount cleanly, then move on to the next section.

Repair Corrupted File Systems

There are a number of scenarios in which a file system might get corrupted through either a hard reboot or some other error. Normally Linux will automatically run a file system check command (called fsck) at boot to attempt to repair the file system. Often the default fsck is enough to repair the file system, but every now and then a file system gets corrupt enough that it needs manual intervention. What you will often see is the boot process drop out after a fsck fails, hopefully to a rescue shell you can use to run fsck manually. Otherwise, track down a rescue disk you can boot from (many distribution install disks double as rescue disks nowadays), open up a terminal window, and make sure you have root permissions (on rescue disks that use sudo, you may have to type sudo -s to get root).

One warning before you start fscking a file system: Be sure the file system is unmounted first. Otherwise fsck could potentially damage your file system further. You can run the mount command in the shell to see all mounted file systems and type umount <devicename> to unmount any that are mounted (except the root file system). Since this file system is preventing you from completing the boot process, it probably isn't mounted, so in this example let's assume that your /home directory is mounted on a separate partition at /dev/sda5. To scan and repair any file system errors on this file system, type

```
# fsck -y -C /dev/sda5
```

The -y option will automatically answer Yes to repair file system errors. Otherwise, if you do have any errors, you will find yourself hitting Y over and over again. The -C option gives you a nice progress bar so you can see how far along fsck is. A complete fsck can take some time on a large file system, so the progress bar can be handy.

Sometimes file systems are so corrupted that the primary superblock cannot be found. Luckily, file systems create backup superblocks in case this happens, so you can tell fsck to use this superblock instead. You aren't likely to automatically know the location of your backup superblock. For ext-based file systems you can use the mke2fs tool with the -n option to list all of the superblocks on a file system:

```
# mke2fs -n /dev/sda5
```

WARNING   Be sure to use the -n option here! Otherwise, mke2fs will simply format your file system and erase all of your old data.

Once you see the list of superblocks in the output, choose one and pass it as an argument to the -b option for fsck:

```
# fsck -b 8193 -y -C /dev/sda5
```

When you specify an alternate superblock, fsck will automatically update your primary superblock after it completes the file system check.

Repair Software RAID

The hard drive is one of the pieces of hardware most likely to break on your server, and if you run a system that uses Linux software RAID, it's good to know how to repair the RAID. The first step is figuring out how to detect when a RAID has failed. On a modern software RAID install, the system should have mdadm configured to email the root user whenever there is a RAID problem (if you want to change this, edit the MAILADDR option in /etc/mdadm/mdadm.conf and run /etc/init.d/mdadm reload as root to load the changes). Otherwise you can view the /proc/mdstat file:

```
$ cat /proc/mdstat
Personalities : [linear] [multipath] [raid0] [raid1] [raid6]
```

```
[raid5] [raid4] [raid10]
md0 : active raid5 sdb1[0] sdd1[3](F) sdc1[1]
16771584 blocks level 5, 64k chunk, algorithm 2 [3/2] [UU_]
unused devices: <none>
```

Here you can see that sdd1 is marked with an (F) stating it has failed, and on the next line of output, the array shows two out of three disks ([3/2] [UU_]). The next step is to remove the disk from /dev/md0 so that you can swap it out with a new drive. To do this, run mdadm with the --remove option:

```
$ sudo mdadm /dev/md0 --remove /dev/sdd1
```

The drive must be set as a failed drive for you to remove it, so if for some reason mdadm hasn't picked up the drive as faulty but you want to swap it out, you might need to set it as faulty before you remove it:

```
$ sudo mdadm /dev/md0 --fail /dev/sdd1
```

The mdadm command supports chaining commands, so you could fail and remove a drive in the same line:

```
$ sudo mdadm /dev/md0 --fail /dev/sdd1 --remove /dev/sdd1
```

Once you remove a drive from an array, it will be missing from /proc/ mdstat:

```
$ cat /prod/mdstat
Personalities : [linear] [multipath] [raid0] [raid1] [raid6]
[raid5] [raid4] [raid10]
md0 : active raid5 sdb1[0] sdc1[1]
16771584 blocks level 5, 64k chunk, algorithm 2 [3/2] [UU_]
unused devices: <none>
```

Now you can swap out the drive with a fresh one and partition it (either a hot-swap if your system supports that, or otherwise by powering the system down and swapping the hard drives). Be sure that when you replace drives you create new partitions to be equal or greater in size than the rest of the partitions in the RAID array. Once the new partition is ready, use the --add command to add it to the array:

```
$ sudo mdadm /dev/md0 --add /dev/sdd1
```

Now mdadm will start the process of resyncing data. This can take some time, depending on the speed and size of your disks. You can monitor the progress from /proc/mdstat:

```
$ cat /proc/mdstat
Personalities : [linear] [multipath] [raid0] [raid1] [raid6]
[raid5] [raid4] [raid10]
md0 : active raid5 sdd1[3] sdb1[0] sdc1[1]
16771584 blocks level 5, 64k chunk, algorithm 2 [3/2] [UU_]
[>....................] recovery = 2.0% (170112/8385792)
finish=1.6min speed=85056K/sec
unused devices: <none>
```

NOTE   If you get tired of running cat /proc/mdstat over and over, you can use the watch command to update it every few seconds. For instance, to run that command every 5 seconds you could type

```
$ watch -n 5 "cat /proc/mdstat"
```

Just hit Ctrl-C to exit out of the watch command when you are done.

## CHAPTER 5

Is the Server Down?
Tracking Down the Source
of Network Problems

MOST SERVERS ARE ATTACHED to some sort of network and generally use the network to provide some sort of service. Many different problems can creep up on a network, so network troubleshooting skills become crucial for anyone responsible for servers or services on those servers. Linux provides a large set of network troubleshooting tools, and this chapter discusses a few common network problems along with how to use some of the tools available for Linux to track down the root cause.

Network troubleshooting skills are invaluable for every member of a DevOps team. It's almost a given that software will communicate over the network in some way, and in many applications, network connectivity is absolutely vital for the software to function. When there is a problem with the network, everyone from the sysadmin, to the QA team, to the entire development staff will probably take notice. Whether your networking department is a separate group or not, when your entire DevOps team works together on diagnosing networking problems, you will get a better overall view of the problem. Your development team will give you the deep knowledge of how your software operates on the network; your QA team will explain how the application behaves under unusual circumstances and provide you with a backlog of networking bug history; and your sysadmin will provide you with an overall perspective of how networked applications work under Linux. Together you will be able to diagnose networking problems much faster than any team can individually.

Server A Can't Talk to Server B

Probably the most common network troubleshooting scenario involves one server being unable to communicate with another server on the network. This section will use an example in which a server named dev1 can't access the web service (port 80) on a second server named web1. Any number of different problems could cause this, so we'll run step by step through tests you can perform to isolate the cause of the problem.

Normally when troubleshooting a problem like this, you might skip a few of these initial steps (such as checking the link), since tests further down the line will also rule them out. For instance, if you test and confirm that DNS works, you've proven that your host can communicate on the local network. For this example, though, we'll walk through each intermediary step to illustrate how you might test each level.

Client or Server Problem

One quick test you can perform to narrow down the cause of your problem is to go to another host on the same network and try to access the server. In this example, you would find another server on the same network as dev1, such as dev2, and try to access web1. If dev2 also can't access web1, then you know the problem is more likely on web1, or on the network between dev1, dev2, and web1. If dev2 can access web1, then you know the problem is more likely on dev1. To start, let's assume that dev2 can access web1, so we will focus our troubleshooting on dev1.

Is It Plugged In?

The first troubleshooting steps to perform are on the client. You first want to verify that your client's connection to the network is healthy. To do this you can use the ethtool program (installed via the ethtool package) to verify that your link is up (the Ethernet device is physically connected to the network). If you aren't sure what interface you use, run the /sbin/ifconfig command to list all the available network interfaces and their settings. So if your Ethernet device was at eth0

```
$ sudo ethtool eth0
Settings for eth0:
     Supported ports: [ TP ]
     Supported link modes:   10baseT/Half 10baseT/Full
                             100baseT/Half 100baseT/Full
                             1000baseT/Half 1000baseT/Full
     Supports auto-negotiation: Yes
     Advertised link modes:  10baseT/Half 10baseT/Full
                             100baseT/Half 100baseT/Full
                             1000baseT/Half 1000baseT/Full
     Advertised auto-negotiation: Yes
     Speed: 100Mb/s
     Duplex: Full
     Port: Twisted Pair
     PHYAD: 0
     Transceiver: internal
```

```
Auto-negotiation: on
Supports Wake-on: pg
Wake-on: d
Current message level: 0x000000ff (255)
Link detected: yes
```

Here, on the final line, you can see that Link detected is set to yes, so dev1 is physically connected to the network. If this was set to no, you would need to physically inspect dev1's network connection and make sure it was connected. Since it is physically connected, you can move on.

NOTE   ethtool has uses beyond simply checking for a link. It can also be used to diagnose and correct duplex issues. When a Linux server connects to a network, typically it autonegotiates with the network to see what speeds it can use and whether the network supports full duplex. The Speed and Duplex lines in the example ethtool output illustrate what a 100Mb/s, full duplex network should report. If you notice slow network speeds on a host, its speed and duplex settings are a good place to look. Run ethtool as in the previous example, and if you notice Duplex set to Half, then run

```
$ sudo ethtool -s eth0 autoneg off duplex full
```

Replace eth0 with your Ethernet device.

Is the Interface Up?

Once you have established that you are physically connected to the network, the next step is to confirm that the network interface is configured correctly on your host. The best way to check this is to run the ifconfig command with your interface as an argument. So to test eth0's settings, you would run

```
$ sudo ifconfig eth0
eth0      Link encap:Ethernet  HWaddr 00:17:42:1f:18:be
          inet addr:10.1.1.7  Bcast:10.1.1.255  Mask:255.255.255.0
          inet6 addr: fe80::217:42ff:fe1f:18be/64 Scope:Link
          UP BROADCAST MULTICAST  MTU:1500  Metric:1
          RX packets:1 errors:0 dropped:0 overruns:0 frame:0
          TX packets:11 errors:0 dropped:0 overruns:0 carrier:0
          collisions:0 txqueuelen:1000
          RX bytes:229 (229.0 B)  TX bytes:2178 (2.1 KB)
          Interrupt:10
```

Probably the most important line in this is the second line of output, which tells us our host has an IP address (10.1.1.7) and subnet mask (255.255.255.0) configured. Now, whether these are the correct settings for this host is something you will need to confirm. If the interface is not configured, try running sudo ifup eth0 and then run ifconfig again to see if the interface comes up. If the settings are wrong or the interface won't come up, inspect /etc/network/interfaces on Debian-based systems or /etc/sysconfig/network_scripts/ifcfg-<interface> on Red Hat-based systems. It is in these files that you can correct any errors in the network settings. Now if the host gets its IP through DHCP, you will need to move your trouble-shooting to the DHCP host to find out why you aren't getting a lease.

Is It on the Local Network?

Once you see that the interface is up, the next step is to see if a default gate-way has been set and whether you can access it. The route command will display your current routing table, including your default gateway:

```
$ sudo route -n
Kernel IP routing table
Destination     Gateway         Genmask         Flags Metric Ref    Use Iface
10.1.1.0        *               255.255.255.0   U     0      0        0 eth0
default         10.1.1.1        0.0.0.0         UG    100    0        0 eth0
```

The line you are interested in is the last line, which starts with default. Here you can see that the host has a gateway of 10.1.1.1. Note that the -n option was used with route so it wouldn't try to resolve any of these IP addresses into hostnames. For one thing, the command runs more quickly, but more important, you don't want to cloud your troubleshooting with any potential DNS errors. If you don't see a default gateway configured here, and the host you want to reach is on a different subnet (say, web1, which is on 10.1.2.5), that is the likely cause of your problem. To fix this, either be sure to set the gateway in /etc/network/interfaces on Debian-based systems or /etc/sysconfig/network_scripts/ifcfg-<interface> on Red Hat-based systems, or if you get your IP via DHCP, be sure it is set correctly on the DHCP server and then reset your interface with the following on Debian-based systems:

```
$ sudo service networking restart
```

The following would be used on Red Hat-based systems:

```
$ sudo service network restart
```

On a side note, it's amazing that these distributions have to differ even on something this fundamental.

Once you have identified the gateway, use the ping command to confirm that you can communicate with the gateway:

```
$ ping -c 5 10.1.1.1
PING 10.1.1.1 (10.1.1.1) 56(84) bytes of data.
64 bytes from 10.1.1.1: icmp_seq=1 ttl=64 time=3.13 ms
64 bytes from 10.1.1.1: icmp_seq=2 ttl=64 time=1.43 ms
64 bytes from 10.1.1.1: icmp_seq=3 ttl=64 time=1.79 ms
64 bytes from 10.1.1.1: icmp_seq=5 ttl=64 time=1.50 ms
--- 10.1.1.1 ping statistics ---
5 packets transmitted, 4 received, 20% packet loss, time 4020ms
rtt min/avg/max/mdev = 1.436/1.966/3.132/0.686 ms
```

As you can see, we were able to successfully ping the gateway, which means that we can at least communicate with the 10.1.1.0 network. If you couldn't ping the gateway, it could mean a few things. It could mean that your gateway is blocking ICMP packets. If so, tell your network administrator that blocking ICMP is an annoying practice with negligible security benefits and then try to ping another Linux host on the same subnet. If ICMP isn't being blocked, then it's possible that the switch port on your host is set to the wrong VLAN, so you will need to further inspect the switch to which it is connected.

Is DNS Working?

Once you have confirmed that you can speak to the gateway, the next thing to test is whether DNS functions. Both the nslookup and dig tools can be used to troubleshoot DNS issues, but since you need to perform only basic testing at this point, just use nslookup to see if you can resolve web1 into an IP:

```
$ nslookup web1
Server: 10.1.1.3
Address: 10.1.1.3#53
```

```
Name: web1.example.net
Address: 10.1.2.5
```

In this example DNS is working. The web1 host expands into web1.example.net and resolves to the address 10.1.2.5. Of course, make sure that this IP matches the IP that web1 is supposed to have! In this case, DNS works, so we can move on to the next section; however, there are also a number of ways DNS could fail.

No Name Server Configured or Inaccessible Name Server   If you see the following error, it could mean either that you have no name servers configured for your host or they are inaccessible:

```
$ nslookup web1
;; connection timed out; no servers could be reached
```

In either case you will need to inspect /etc/resolv.conf and see if any name servers are configured there. If you don't see any IP addresses configured there, you will need to add a name server to the file. Otherwise, if you see something like the following, you need to start troubleshooting your connection with your name server, starting off with ping:

```
search example.net
nameserver 10.1.1.3
```

If you can't ping the name server and its IP address is in the same subnet (in this case, 10.1.1.3 is within the subnet), the name server itself could be completely down. If you can't ping the name server and its IP address is in a different subnet, then skip ahead to the Can I Route to the Remote Host? section, but only apply those troubleshooting steps to the name server's IP. If you can ping the name server but it isn't responding, skip ahead to the Is the Remote Port Open? section.

Missing Search Path or Name Server Problem   It is also possible that you will get the following error for your nslookup command:

```
$ nslookup web1
Server: 10.1.1.3
```

```
Address: 10.1.1.3#53
** server can't find web1: NXDOMAIN
```

Here you see that the server did respond, since it gave a response: server can't find web1. This could mean two different things. One, it could mean that web1's domain name is not in your DNS search path. This is set in /etc/resolv.conf in the line that begins with search. A good way to test this is to perform the same nslookup command, only use the fully qualified domain name (in this case, web1.example.net). If it does resolve, then either always use the fully qualified domain name, or if you want to be able to use just the hostname, add the domain name to the search path in /etc/resolv.conf.

If even the fully qualified domain name doesn't resolve, then the problem is on the name server. The complete method for troubleshooting all DNS issues is covered in Chapter 6, but here are some basic pointers. If the name server is supposed to have that record, then that zone's configuration needs to be examined. If it is a recursive name server, then you will have to test whether or not recursion is working on the name server by looking up some other domain. If you can look up other domains, then you must check if the problem is on the remote name server that does contain the zones.

Can I Route to the Remote Host?

After you have ruled out DNS issues and see that web1 is resolved into its IP 10.1.2.5, you must test whether you can route to the remote host. Assuming ICMP is enabled on your network, one quick test might be to ping web1. If you can ping the host, you know your packets are being routed there and you can move to the next section, Is the Remote Port Open? If you can't ping web1, try to identify another host on that network and see if you can ping it. If you can, then it's possible web1 is down or blocking your requests, so move to the next section. If you can't ping any hosts on the remote network, packets aren't being routed correctly. One of the best tools to test routing issues is traceroute. Once you provide traceroute with a host, it will test each hop between you and the host. For example, a successful traceroute between dev1 and web1 would look like this:

```
$ traceroute 10.1.2.5
traceroute to 10.1.2.5 (10.1.2.5), 30 hops max, 40 byte packets
1 10.1.1.1 (10.1.1.1) 5.432 ms 5.206 ms 5.472 ms
2 web1 (10.1.2.5) 8.039 ms 8.348 ms 8.643 ms
```

Here you can see that packets go from dev1 to its gateway (10.1.1.1), and then the next hop is web1. This means it's likely that 10.1.1.1 is the gateway for both subnets. On your network you might see a slightly different output if there are more routers between you and your host. If you can't ping web1, your output would look more like the following:

```
$ traceroute 10.1.2.5
traceroute to 10.1.2.5 (10.1.2.5), 30 hops max, 40 byte packets
1 10.1.1.1 (10.1.1.1) 5.432 ms 5.206 ms 5.472 ms
2 * * *
3 * * *
```

Once you start seeing asterisks in your output, you know that the problem is on your gateway. You will need to go to that router and investigate why it can't route packets between the two networks. Instead you might see something more like

```
$ traceroute 10.1.2.5
traceroute to 10.1.2.5 (10.1.2.5), 30 hops max, 40 byte packets
1 10.1.1.1 (10.1.1.1) 5.432 ms 5.206 ms 5.472 ms
1 10.1.1.1 (10.1.1.1) 3006.477 ms !H 3006.779 ms !H 3007.072 ms
```

In this case, you know that the ping timed out at the gateway, so the host is likely down or inaccessible even from the same subnet. At this point, if you haven't tried to access web1 from a machine on the same subnet as web1, try pings and other tests now.

NOTE   If you have one of those annoying networks that block ICMP, don't worry, you can still troubleshoot routing issues. You just need to install the tcptraceroute package (sudo apt-get install tcptraceroute), then run the same commands as for traceroute, only substitute tcptraceroute for traceroute.

Is the Remote Port Open?

So you can route to the machine but you still can't access the web server on port 80. The next test is to see whether the port is even open. There are a number of different ways to do this. For one, you could try telnet:

```
$ telnet 10.1.2.5 80
Trying 10.1.2.5...
telnet: Unable to connect to remote host: Connection refused
```

If you see Connection refused, then either the port is down (likely Apache isn't running on the remote host or isn't listening on that port) or the firewall is blocking your access. If telnet can connect, then, well, you don't have a networking problem at all. If the web service isn't working the way you suspected, you need to investigate your Apache configuration on web1. Troubleshooting web server issues is covered in Chapter 8.

Instead of telnet, I prefer to use nmap to test ports because it can often detect firewalls. If nmap isn't installed, use your package manager to install the nmap package. To test web1, type the following:

```
$ nmap -p 80 10.1.2.5
Starting Nmap 4.62 ( http://nmap.org ) at 2009-02-05 18:49 PST
Interesting ports on web1 (10.1.2.5):
PORT STATE SERVICE
80/tcp filtered http
```

Aha! nmap is smart enough that it can often tell the difference between a closed port that is truly closed and a closed port behind a firewall. Normally when a port is actually down, nmap will report it as closed. Here it reported it as filtered. What this tells us is that some firewall is in the way and is dropping the packets to the floor. This means you need to investigate any firewall rules on the gateway (10.1.1.1) and on web1 itself to see if port 80 is being blocked.

Test the Remote Host Locally

At this point, we have either been able to narrow the problem down to a network issue or we believe the problem is on the host itself. If we think the problem is on the host itself, we can do a few things to test whether port 80 is available.

Test for Listening Ports

One of the first things you should do on web1 is test whether port 80 is listening. The netstat -lnp command will list all ports that are listening along with the process that has the port open. You could just run that and parse through the output for anything that is listening on port 80, or you could use grep to show only things listening on port 80:

```
$ sudo netstat -lnp | grep :80
tcp 0 0 0.0.0.0:80 0.0.0.0:* LISTEN 919/apache
```

The first column tells you what protocol the port is using. The second and third columns are the receive and send queues (both are set to 0 here). The column you want to pay attention to is the fourth column, as it lists the local address on which the host is listening. Here the 0.0.0.0:80 tells us that the host is listening on all of its IPs for port 80 traffic. If Apache were listening only on web1's Ethernet address, you would see 10.1.2.5:80 here.

The final column will tell you which process has the port open. Here you can see that Apache is running and listening. If you do not see this in your netstat output, you need to start your Apache server.

Firewall Rules

If the process is running and listening on port 80, it's possible that web1 has some sort of firewall in place. Use the iptables command to list all of your firewall rules. If your firewall is disabled, your output will look like this:

```
$ sudo /sbin/iptables -L
Chain INPUT (policy ACCEPT)
target     prot opt source            destination

Chain FORWARD (policy ACCEPT)
target     prot opt source            destination

Chain OUTPUT (policy ACCEPT)
target     prot opt source            destination
```

Notice that the default policy is set to ACCEPT. It's possible, though, that your firewall is set to drop all packets by default, even if it doesn't list any rules. If that is the case you will see output more like the following:

```
$ sudo /sbin/iptables -L
Chain INPUT (policy DROP)
target     prot opt source              destination

Chain FORWARD (policy DROP)
target     prot opt source              destination

Chain OUTPUT (policy DROP)
target     prot opt source              destination
```

On the other hand, if you had a firewall rule that blocked port 80, it might look like this:

```
$ sudo /sbin/iptables -L -n
Chain INPUT (policy ACCEPT)
target     prot opt source              destination
REJECT     tcp  --  0.0.0.0/0           0.0.0.0/0         tcp dpt:80 reject-with
   ↪icmp-port-unreachable

Chain FORWARD (policy ACCEPT)
target     prot opt source              destination

Chain OUTPUT (policy ACCEPT)
target     prot opt source              destination
```

Clearly, in the latter case you would need to modify the firewall rules to allow port 80 traffic from the host.

Troubleshoot Slow Networks

In a way, it's easier to troubleshoot network problems when something doesn't work at all. When a host is unreachable, you can perform the troubleshooting steps discussed earlier until the host is reachable again. When the network is just slow, however, sometimes it can be a bit tricky to track down why. This section discusses a few techniques you can use to track down the cause of slow networks.

DNS Issues

Although DNS is blamed more often than it should be for network problems, when DNS does have an issue, it can often result in poor network performance. For instance, if you have two DNS servers configured for a domain and the first one you try goes down, your DNS requests will wait 30 seconds before they time out and go to the secondary DNS server. Although this will definitely be noticeable when you run tools like dig or nslookup, DNS issues can cause apparent network slowdowns in some unexpected ways; this is because so many services rely on DNS to resolve hostnames to IP addresses. Such issues can even affect your network troubleshooting tools.

Ping, traceroute, route, netstat, and even iptables are great examples of network troubleshooting tools that can degrade during DNS issues. By default, all of these tools will attempt to resolve IP addresses into hostnames if they can. If there are DNS problems, however, the results from each of these commands might stall while they attempt to look up IP addresses and fail. In the case of ping or traceroute, it might seem like your ping replies are taking a long time, yet when they do finally come through, the round-trip time is relatively low. In the case of route, netstat, and iptables, the results might stall for quite some time before you get output. The system is waiting for DNS requests to time out.

In all of the cases mentioned, it's easy to bypass DNS so your troubleshooting results are accurate. All of the commands we discussed earlier accept an -n option, which disables any attempt to resolve IP addresses into hostnames. I've just become accustomed to adding -n to all of the commands I introduced you to in the first part of this chapter unless I really do want IP addresses resolved.

NOTE   Although we'll get into this more in Chapter 8, DNS resolution can also affect your web server's performance in an unexpected way. Some web servers are configured to resolve every IP address that accesses them into a hostname for logging. Although that can make the logs more readable, it can also dramatically slow down your web server at the worst times—when you have a lot of visitors. Instead of serving traffic, your web server can get busy trying to resolve all of those IPs.

Find the Network Slowdown with traceroute

When your network connection seems slow between your server and a host on a different network, sometimes it can be difficult to track down where the real slowdown is. Especially in situations where the slowdown is in latency (the time it takes to get a response) and not overall bandwidth, it's a situation traceroute was made for. traceroute was mentioned earlier in the chapter as a way to test overall connectivity between you and a server on a remote network, but traceroute is also useful when you need to diagnose where a network slowdown might be. Since traceroute outputs the reply times for every hop between you and another machine, you can trace down servers that might be on a different continent or gateways that might be overloaded and causing network slowdowns. For instance, here's part of a traceroute between a server in the United States and a Chinese Yahoo server:

```
$ traceroute yahoo.cn
traceroute to yahoo.cn (202.165.102.205), 30 hops max, 60 byte packets
 1  64-142-56-169.static.sonic.net (64.142.56.169)  1.666 ms  2.351 ms  3.038 ms
 2  2.ge-1-1-0.gw.sr.sonic.net (209.204.191.36)  1.241 ms  1.243 ms  1.229 ms
 3  265.ge-7-1-0.gw.paol.sonic.net (64.142.0.198)  3.388 ms  3.612 ms  3.592 ms
 4  xe-1-0-6.ar1.paol.us.nlayer.net (69.22.130.85)  6.464 ms  6.607 ms  6.642 ms
 5  ae0-80g.cr1.paol.us.nlayer.net (69.22.153.18)  3.320 ms  3.404 ms  3.496 ms
 6  ae1-50g.cr1.sjcl.us.nlayer.net (69.22.143.165)  4.335 ms  3.955 ms  3.957 ms
 7  ae1-40g.ar2.sjcl.us.nlayer.net (69.22.143.118)  8.748 ms  5.500 ms  7.657 ms
 8  as4837.xe-4-0-2.ar2.sjcl.us.nlayer.net (69.22.153.146)  3.864 ms  3.863 ms  3.865 ms
 9  219.158.30.177 (219.158.30.177)  275.648 ms  275.702 ms  275.687 ms
10  219.158.97.117 (219.158.97.117)  284.506 ms  284.552 ms  262.416 ms
11  219.158.97.93 (219.158.97.93)  263.538 ms  270.178 ms  270.121 ms
12  219.158.4.65 (219.158.4.65)  303.441 ms  *  303.465 ms
13  202.96.12.190 (202.96.12.190)  306.968 ms  306.971 ms  307.052 ms
14  61.148.143.10 (61.148.143.10)  295.916 ms  295.780 ms  295.860 ms
...
```

Without knowing much about the network, you can assume just by looking at the round-trip times that once you get to hop 9 (at the 219.158.30.177 IP), you have left the continent, as the round-trip time jumps from 3 milliseconds to 275 milliseconds.

Find What Is Using Your Bandwidth with iftop

Sometimes your network is slow not because of some problem on a remote server or router, but just because something on the system is using up all the available bandwidth. It can be tricky to identify what process is using up all the bandwidth, but there are some tools you can use to help identify the culprit.

top is such a great troubleshooting tool that it has inspired a number of similar tools like iotop to identify what processes are consuming the most disk I/O. It turns out there is a tool called iftop that does something similar with network connections. Unlike top, iftop doesn't concern itself with processes but instead lists the connections between your server and a remote IP that are consuming the most bandwidth (Figure 5-1). For instance, with iftop you can quickly see if your backup job is using up all your bandwidth by seeing the backup server IP address at the top of the output.

iftop is available in a package of the same name on both Red Hat- and Debian-based distributions, but in the case of Red Hat-based distributions,

	12.5Kb	25.0Kb	37.5Kb	50.0Kb	62.5Kb
64.142.56.172	=> 70.240.180.184		819Kb	199Kb	125Kb
	<=		44.9Kb	10.9Kb	6.82Kb
64.142.56.172	=> 66.249.67.235		0b	5.55Kb	3.47Kb
	<=		0b	861b	538b
64.142.56.172	=> 75.101.46.232		4.39Kb	2.66Kb	2.55Kb
	<=		208b	250b	312b
64.142.56.172	=> 75.101.59.150		0b	298b	186b
	<=		160b	419b	262b
64.142.56.172	=> 151.164.11.205		0b	408b	255b
	<=		0b	234b	146b
64.142.56.172	=> 89.16.176.16		0b	145b	99b
	<=		0b	227b	142b
64.142.56.172	=> 69.227.255.40		0b	204b	128b
	<=		0b	117b	73b
64.142.56.172	=> 95.129.184.129		0b	210b	132b
	<=		0b	107b	67b
64.142.56.172	=> 74.125.52.95		0b	142b	89b
	<=		0b	66b	41b
TX: cumm: 263KB peak: 823Kb rates:			823Kb	209Kb	132Kb
RX: 17.1KB 45.3Kb			45.3Kb	13.3Kb	8.53Kb
TOTAL: 280KB 868Kb			868Kb	223Kb	140Kb

Figure 5-1 Sample iftop output

you might have to find it from a third-party repository. Once you have it installed, just run the iftop command on the command line (it will require root permissions). Like with the top command, you can hit Q to quit.

At the very top of the iftop screen is a bar that shows the overall traffic for the interface. Just below that is a column with source IPs followed by a column with destination IPs and arrows between them so you can see whether the bandwidth is being used to transmit packets from your host or receive them from the remote host. After those columns are three more columns that represent the data rate between the two hosts over 2, 10, and 40 seconds, respectively. Much like with load averages, you can see whether the bandwidth is spiking now, or has spiked some time in the past. At the very bottom of the screen, you can see statistics for transmitted data (TX) and received data (RX) along with totals. Like with top, the interface updates periodically.

The iftop command run with no arguments at all is often all you need for your troubleshooting, but every now and then, you may want to take advantage of some of its options. The iftop command will show statistics for the first interface it can find by default, but on some servers you may have multiple interfaces, so if you wanted to run iftop against your second Ethernet interface (eth1), type iftop -i eth1.

By default iftop attempts to resolve all IP addresses into hostnames. One downside to this is that it can slow down your reporting if a remote DNS server is slow. Another downside is that all that DNS resolution adds extra network traffic that might show up in iftop! To disable network resolution, just run iftop with the -n option.

Normally iftop displays overall bandwidth used between hosts, but to help you narrow things down, you might want to see what ports each host is using to communicate. After all, if you knew a host was consuming most of your bandwidth over your web port, you would perform different troubleshooting than if it was connecting to an FTP port. Once iftop is launched, press P to toggle between displaying all ports and hiding them. One thing you'll notice, though, is that sometimes displaying all the ports can cause hosts you are interested in to fall off the screen. If that happens, you can also hit either S or D to toggle between displaying ports only from the source or only from the destination host, respectively. Showing only source ports can be useful when you run iftop on a server, since for many services, the destination host uses random high ports that don't necessarily identify what service is being used, but the ports on your server are more likely to correspond to a service on your machine. You can then follow up with the netstat -lnp command referenced earlier in this chapter to find out what service is listening on that port.

Like with most Linux commands, iftop has an advanced range of options. What we covered should be enough to help with most troubleshooting efforts, but in case you want to dig further into iftop's capabilities, just type man iftop to read the manual included with the package.

Packet Captures

Although the techniques mentioned in this chapter should help you troubleshoot a wide range of networking problems, some problems are so subtle or low-level that the only way to track them down is to dig down into the protocol itself and examine individual packets as they go back and forth. Because of the low-level and tedious nature of analyzing packet dumps, you should try to use it as a last resort. That said, this type of troubleshooting can be quite effective, particularly to identify hosts on your local network that are misbehaving, hosts with misconfigured network settings, or debugging communications between your own client and server software. Packet dumps are less effective for troubleshooting if you are unfamiliar with the protocols you are examining since you can't tell correct traffic from errors, or if you allow yourself to get buried in volumes of packets and can't see the problem for all of the normal traffic.

When you capture packets, it's most effective if you can capture them on both sides of a communication, especially if there is a router or firewall between two hosts. If a machine between the two hosts is the cause of the problem, you're more likely to detect it when you can see whether packets sent from host A arrive on host B exactly as they are sent. For instance, if you see host B send a reply back to host A that never gets there, you can be confident that the problem is somewhere in between the two hosts.

A great example of where packet captures come into play occurred some time back when I was troubleshooting a host that seemed to have trouble communicating with a different server. Connections would sometimes just die out, yet at other times things seemed relatively fine, if slow. Nothing can be trickier to troubleshoot than an intermittent problem. After a series of different troubleshooting steps, we captured packets both from the problem host and the destination server.

What we discovered in the packet dump was that a misconfigured router had been trying to apply NAT (Network Address Translation) rules to our destination server incorrectly and had sent reply packets back to our host while the destination server was trying to reply to us directly. Our host was seeing the same reply twice, but from two different MAC addresses. What happened was a race where each time we tried to set up a TCP handshake, sometimes the destination server won the race and replied back, but other times the router replied back first; upon seeing that reply, our host tried to re-initiate the handshake. Depending on who won the race, the communication would continue or get reset. If we weren't able to analyze the individual packets going back and forth, we may have never discovered the duplicate packets.

Use the tcpdump Tool

The main packet capture tool we will discuss is tcpdump. This is an old and proven command-line packet capture tool, and although there are more modern tools out there, tcpdump is a program that you should be able to find on any Linux system. Because of how tcpdump works, you will need to run it with root privileges on your machine. By default, it will scan through your network interfaces and choose the first suitable one; then it will capture, parse, and output information about the packets it sees. Here's some example output from tcpdump with the -n option (so it doesn't convert IP addresses to hostnames and slow things down):

```
$ sudo tcpdump -n
tcpdump: verbose output suppressed, use -v or -vv for full protocol decode
listening on eth0, link-type EN10MB (Ethernet), capture size 96 bytes
19:01:51.133159 IP 208.115.111.75.60004 > 64.142.56.172.80: Flags [F.], seq 753858968, ack
  ↪1834304357, win 272, options [nop,nop,TS val 99314435 ecr 1766147273], length 0
```

```
19:01:51.133317 IP 64.142.56.172.80 > 208.115.111.75.60004: Flags [F.], seq 1, ack 1, win
↪54, options [nop,nop,TS val 1766147276 ecr 99314435], length 0
19:01:51.157772 IP 208.115.111.75.60004 > 64.142.56.172.80: Flags [.], ack 2, win 272,
↪options [nop,nop,TS val 99314437 ecr 1766147276], length 0
19:01:51.224021 IP 72.240.13.35.45665 > 64.142.56.172.53: 59454% [1au] AAAA? ns2.example.
↪net. (45)
19:01:51.224510 IP 64.142.56.172.53 > 72.240.13.35.45665: 59454*- 0/1/1 (90)
19:01:51.256743 IP 201.52.186.78.63705 > 64.142.56.172.80: Flags [.], ack 1833085614, win
↪65340, length 0
```

NOTE Whenever you are done capturing packets, just hit Ctrl-C to exit tcpdump. As tcpdump exits, it tells you how many packets it was able to capture and how many the kernel dropped.

The output of tcpdump can be a bit tricky to parse at first, and I won't go over all the columns, but let's take two lines from the preceding output and break them down:

```
19:01:51.224021 IP 72.240.13.35.45665 > 64.142.56.172.53: 59454% [1au] AAAA? ns2.example.
↪net. (45)
19:01:51.224510 IP 64.142.56.172.53 > 72.240.13.35.45665: 59454*- 0/1/1 (90)
```

The first line tells you that at 19:01:51, the host 72.240.13.35 on port 45665 sent a packet to 64.142.56.172 on port 53 (DNS). If you wanted to dig further in that line you could see that the source host sent a request for the AAAA record (an IPv6 IP address) for ns2.example.net. The second line tells you that also at 19:01:51 the host 64.142.56.172 on port 53 replied back to host 72.240.13.35 on port 45665, presumably with an answer to the query.

Since the first column is a datestamp for each packet, it makes it simple to see how long communication takes between hosts. This can be particularly useful for protocols that have set timeouts (like 30-second timeouts for DNS requests) since you can watch the timeout occur and see the source host resend its request. The next major column shows the IP and port for the source host. The > in the line can be treated like an arrow that lets you know that the direction of communication is from the first IP to the

second. Finally, the next column tells you the destination IP and port followed by some extra flags, sequence numbers, and other TCP/IP information for that packet that we won't get into here.

Filtering Tcpdump Output   Since by default tcpdump captures all of the
packets it sees, it usually bombards you with a lot of noise that doesn't
help with your troubleshooting. What you want to do is pass tcpdump some
filtering rules so it only shows you packets that you are interested in. For
instance, if you were troubleshooting problems between your host and a
server with a hostname of web1, you could tell tcpdump to only show packets
to or from that host with

```
$ sudo tcpdump -n host web1
```

If you wanted to do the opposite, that is, show all traffic except anything
from web1, you would say

```
$ sudo tcpdump -n not host web1
```

You can also filter traffic to and from specific ports. For instance, if you
wanted to just see DNS traffic (port 53) you would type

```
$ sudo tcpdump -n port 53
```

If you wanted to capture all of your web traffic on either port 80 or port
443, you would type

```
$ sudo tcpdump -n port 80 or port 443
```

You can actually get rather sophisticated with tcpdump filters, but it's often
easier to just capture a certain level of tcpdump output to a file and then use
grep or other tools to filter it further. To save tcpdump output to a file, you can
use a command-line redirect:

```
$ sudo tcpdump -n host web1 > outputfile
```

If you want to view the packets on the command line while they are being saved to a file, add the -l option to tcpdump so it buffers the output, and then use tee to both display the output and save it to a file:

```
$ sudo tcpdump -n -l host web1 | tee outputfile
```

Raw Packet Dumps   Although you might think that tcpdump already provides plenty of difficult-to-parse output, sometimes all that output isn't enough—you want to save complete raw packets. Raw packets are particularly useful since they contain absolutely all of the information about communication between hosts, and a number of tools (such as Wireshark, which we'll discuss briefly momentarily) can take these raw packet dumps as input and display them in a much-easier-to-understand way.

The simplest way to save raw packet dumps is to run tcpdump with the -w option:

```
$ sudo tcpdump -w output.pcap
```

Like with other tcpdump commands, hit Ctrl-C to stop capturing packets. You can also use all of the same filtering options we've discussed so far when capturing raw packets. With raw packet dumps, you are getting the complete contents of the packets as best as tcpdump and your disk can keep up. So if someone is transferring a 1Gb file from your server, you might just capture the whole file in your packet dump. You may want to open up a second command-line session just so you can keep an eye on the size of the output file.

tcpdump provides a few options you can use to manage the size of output files. The first option, -C, lets you specify the maximum size of the output file (in millions of bytes) before it moves on to a second one. So, for instance, if you wanted to rotate files after they grow past ten megabytes, you can type

```
$ sudo tcpdump -C 10 -w output.pcap
```

The first output file will be named output.pcap.1, and once it gets to ten megabytes, tcpdump will close it and start writing to output.pcap.2, and so on, until you either kill tcpdump or you run out of disk space. If you want to be sure that you won't run out of disk space, you can also add the -W option, which lets you limit the number of files tcpdump will ultimately create. Once tcpdump reaches the last file, it will start from the beginning and overwrite the first file in the set. So, for instance, if you want tcpdump to rotate to a new file after ten megabytes and want to make sure tcpdump only uses fifty megabytes of disk space, you could limit it to five rotated files:

```
$ sudo tcpdump -C 10 -W 5 -w output.pcap
```

Once you have these packet captures, you can use tcpdump to replay them as though they were happening in real time with the -r option. Just specify your raw packet output file as an argument. You can specify filters and other options like -n just as if you were running tcpdump against a live stream of traffic:

```
$ sudo tcpdump -n -r output.pcap
```

The tcpdump program is full of useful options and filters beyond what I've mentioned here. The man page (type man tcpdump) not only goes over all of these options and filters, but it also provides a nice primer on TCP packet construction, so it's worth looking through if you want to dig deeper into tcpdump's abilities.

Use Wireshark

Although tcpdump is a handy tool for packet capture, when you actually need to parse through and analyze raw packets, the -r option sometimes doesn't cut it. Luckily some tools make the process simpler. One of the best tools for raw packet analysis is Wireshark. It is a desktop application that provides a lot of sophisticated tools for packet analysis that are way beyond the scope of this book. At a basic level, though, Wireshark provides you with a much easier way to view your raw packet dumps and pinpoint obvious problems.

The Wireshark package should be packaged and available for major Linux distributions, and it even has clients for Windows and Mac systems. Once installed, you can launch it via your desktop environment or just type wireshark on the command line. If you type wireshark followed by your raw packet file, it will go ahead and open it up as it starts.

As Figure 5-2 shows, Wireshark separates its GUI into a few sections. The main pane below the toolbar displays basic packet information like you might find in default tcpdump output. What's useful about Wireshark is that its columns are a bit simpler to read, plus it color-codes packets based on protocol and will even highlight error packets in red. The color coding in this main pane makes it a bit simpler to filter through your traffic and identify possible problems.

Once you click on a particular packet in the main pane, the pane below it shows all of the detailed information in the different layers of the packet.

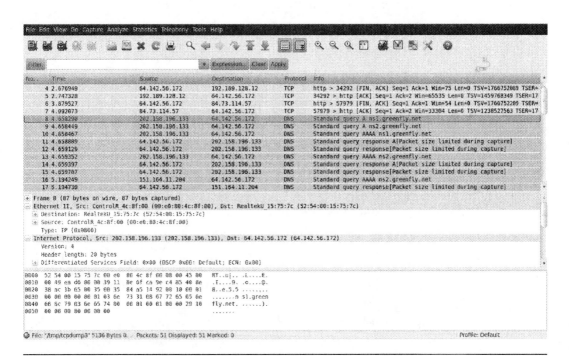

Figure 5-2 Default Wireshark window

In that pane you can drill down to display IP headers, the data section of the packet, and everything in between. Once you do, click on and expand a particular section of a packet; at the very bottom of the window is a separate pane that will show you both the hex and ASCII representation of that data.

Wireshark has a ton of features, including the ability to capture packets in its own right, and is a complicated and powerful-enough tool that it could be a subject for its own book. Since this is a book about troubleshooting and not TCP/IP itself, this section just mentions a few basic features that will help you with troubleshooting.

Along the top toolbar you'll see an input box and a button labeled Filter. As with tcpdump, you filter packet dumps so you only see packets that match your criteria. Unlike tcpdump, Wireshark uses a completely different syntax for filters. So, for instance, if you want to see only packets related to host 192.168.0.1, type this in the filter and press Enter:

```
ip.addr == 192.168.0.1
```

To display only packets related to DNS (port 53), type

```
tcp.port == 53 || udp.port == 53
```

The filtering syntax for Wireshark is pretty extensive, but if you click on the button labeled Filter, a window pops up that gives you a good list of examples to get you started. From there you can also click a Help button that gives you more complete documentation on how to construct your own filter rules.

Another useful feature in Wireshark is the ability to pick a complete stream of communication between two hosts out of a large number of packets. Although you can certainly do this yourself by hand, you can also just select one sample packet you are interested in, then click Analyze → Follow TCP Stream. If it's a UDP or SSL stream, those options will be visible instead. Once you select that menu, a new window pops up (Figure 5-3),

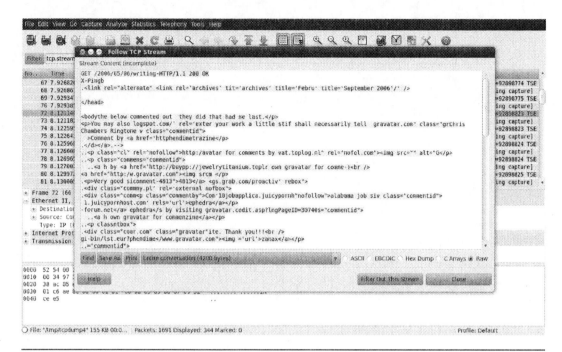

Figure 5-3 Wireshark following an HTTP stream filled with blog spam

and if it is able to piece together any content from that stream, it is displayed. In either case, when you close the Follow TCP Stream window, the main Wireshark window will have automatically filtered out all of the packets except for those related to this particular stream.

## CHAPTER 6

Why Won't the Hostnames Resolve? Solving DNS Server Issues

THE DOMAIN NAME SYSTEM, or DNS, is one of the most important systems on the Internet. Every host on the Internet is assigned an IP address, but most of us don't have the IP addresses of our favorite websites memorized. Instead, we type in a hostname that DNS translates into an IP address behind the scenes. You can also use DNS to convert IP addresses to hostnames. When DNS fails, you end up with an effect much like a failed network connection—you can't reach a website or server you want to reach, but unlike with a failed network connection, your computer and the server are still on the network.

In a DevOps organization, you might be presented with DNS troubleshooting from a number of different areas of responsibility. At the most basic level, you may have no direct control over your DNS system at all, however, you notice you can no longer reach a server you are responsible for or that you develop on, or you may notice your automated tests are timing out when they try to resolve a server name. Ultimately someone else on your team may have to fix the problem, but you want to approach them with some solid data first. Beyond that, perhaps you do manage DNS for a website, but through a registrar or other third party and you really only change records in a web GUI. Now some record you changed didn't update, and you want to sanity-check things before you file a ticket with your DNS provider. Finally, maybe you are a full-fledged DNS administrator running your own DNS server, so when there's a DNS problem, the buck stops with you. No matter where you fit on your DevOps team, DNS troubleshooting skills are valuable to have.

Although understanding how DNS works really helps with troubleshooting, this chapter assumes that your understanding might be a bit hazy. That's OK, because in the process of troubleshooting DNS problems step-by-step in this chapter, we will end up tracing a request all the way through the stack and back. The chapter is split into two distinct parts. The first part talks about how to troubleshoot DNS problems from the client side, and the second part talks about troubleshooting DNS server problems. The client-side troubleshooting will help provide you with the basic troubleshooting steps to know whether the problem is on your end or the DNS server's end. If you do find that the problem is on the server end, the server troubleshooting section will help you trace down some common DNS server issues.

DNS Client Troubleshooting

The first place to troubleshoot DNS problems is on your local host. You will find that even if the problem is on the DNS server side, you can trace down the cause of many DNS server issues from any client with nslookup and dig installed. Both the nslookup and dig tools can be used to trouble-shoot DNS issues, but for basic testing, start with nslookup. For this trouble-shooting step, we'll borrow a scenario from the Chapter 5 where the client has an IP address of 10.1.1.7 and we have a server named web1 that has an IP address of 10.1.2.5 that we want to resolve. Here is an example of a successful nslookup request that resolves web1:

```
$ nslookup web1
Server: 10.1.1.3
Address: 10.1.1.3#53
Name: web1.example.net
Address: 10.1.2.5
```

In this example DNS is working. The web1 host expands into web1.example.net and resolves to the address 10.1.2.5. One of the first things to confirm, of course, is that this IP matches the IP that web1 is supposed to have! If web1 has the wrong IP address, then you can move down to the DNS server troubleshooting section of this chapter to find out why. In this case DNS works; however, there are also a number of ways DNS could fail on the client, ways that give distinct clues.

No Name Server Configured or Inaccessible Name Server

If you see the following error, it could mean that either you have no name servers configured for your host or they are inaccessible:

```
$ nslookup web1
;; connection timed out; no servers could be reached
```

In either case you will need to inspect /etc/resolv.conf and see if any name servers are configured there. If you don't see any IP addresses configured there, you will need to add a name server to the file. Otherwise, you might see something like this:

```
search example.net
nameserver 10.1.1.3
```

You now need to start troubleshooting your connection with your name server, starting off with the ping command. If you can't ping the name server and its IP address is in the same subnet (in this case 10.1.1.3 is within my subnet), the name server itself could be completely down. A good way to confirm this would be to run an nslookup directly against your configured name server by adding its IP address to the command line:

```
$ nslookup web1 10.1.1.3
Server: 10.1.1.3
Address: 10.1.1.3#53
Name: web1.example.net
Address: 10.1.2.5
```

Alternatively, if you want to use dig instead of nslookup, you put @ in front of the name server IP and be sure to use the fully qualified domain name. Also, be ready for a lot more output:

```
$ dig web1.example.net @10.1.1.3
; <<>> DiG 9.7.0-P1 <<>> www.example.net @10.1.1.3
;; global options: +cmd
;; Got answer:
;; ->>HEADER<<- opcode: QUERY, status: NOERROR, id: 23394
;; flags: qr aa rd; QUERY: 1, ANSWER: 1, AUTHORITY: 2, ADDITIONAL: 2
;; WARNING: recursion requested but not available

;; QUESTION SECTION:
;web1.example.net.              IN      A

;; ANSWER SECTION:
web1.example.net.      300      IN      A       10.1.2.5
```

```
;; AUTHORITY SECTION:
example.net.            300     IN      NS      ns2.example.net.
example.net.            300     IN      NS      ns1.example.net.

;; ADDITIONAL SECTION:
ns1.example.net.        300     IN      A       10.1.1.3
ns2.example.net.        300     IN      A       10.1.1.4

;; Query time: 11 msec
;; SERVER: 10.1.1.3#53(10.1.1.3)
;; WHEN: Sat Mar 17 16:56:55 2012
;; MSG SIZE  rcvd: 118
```

Although you could add +short to the end of the dig command to just get the IP address, dig gives us a lot of extra info that is useful for troubleshooting. For instance, it tells us the two name servers for example.net were named ns1 and ns2, and it also gives us their IP addresses. We will use this sort of extra information later when we troubleshoot DNS server issues.

If you can't ping the name server and its IP address is in a different subnet, then either the DNS server is down or you have some kind of networking problem, so you'll want to review Chapter 5, particularly the Can I Route to the Remote Host? section, only apply those troubleshooting steps to the DNS server's IP. If you can ping the name server but it isn't responding, skip ahead to the DNS Server Troubleshooting section of this chapter.

Missing Search Path or Name Server Problem

It is also possible that you will get the following error for your nslookup command:

```
$ nslookup web1
Server: 10.1.1.3
Address: 10.1.1.3#53
** server can't find web1: NXDOMAIN
```

Here you see that the server did respond, since it gave a response server can't find web1. This could mean two different things. One, it could mean that web1's domain name is not in your DNS search path. This is set in

/etc/resolv.conf in the line that begins with search. A good way to test this is to perform the same nslookup command, only use the fully qualified domain name (in this case web1.example.net). If it does resolve, then either always use the fully qualified domain name, or if you want to be able to use just the hostname, add the domain name to the search path in /etc/resolv.conf.

If even the fully qualified domain name doesn't resolve, then the problem is on the name server. The complete method to troubleshoot all DNS issues is covered next, but here are some basic pointers before we dig into that. If the name server is supposed to have that record (i.e., it is configured to be a name server for that domain), then that zone's configuration needs to be examined. If it is a recursive name server, then you will have to test whether recursion is not working on the name server by looking up some other domain. If you can look up other domains, then you must check whether the problem is on the remote name server that does contain the zones. We will cover all of these problems in more detail in the following pages.

DNS Server Troubleshooting

Compared to web, email, and database servers, it seems DNS servers are among the least likely servers one might want to manage themselves. Although it's true that there's a fair learning curve when configuring DNS server software such as BIND, a lot of the reluctance might have to do with the perception that DNS issues are difficult to troubleshoot—they'd rather have someone like a registrar worry about it. This section steps through some of the common problems that plague DNS servers and describes how to best track them down. Even if you don't host your own DNS server and hire it out to someone else, you'll still want to know how to tell whether the problem is on their end!

Understanding dig Output

Although nslookup is a useful tool for DNS troubleshooting, when it comes to DNS servers, I like to use dig. Both tools should be available on your average Linux system, but I like dig for DNS server troubleshooting because of all of the extra information it gives by default. The output from dig is also a lot closer to the actual DNS response from the server, so it helps you learn a bit more about the protocol along the way. Here's some sample dig output as an example:

```
$ dig web1.example.net
; <<>> DiG 9.7.0-P1 <<>> example.net
;; global options: +cmd
;; Got answer:
;; ->>HEADER<<- opcode: QUERY, status: NOERROR, id: 30750
;; flags: qr aa rd ra; QUERY: 1, ANSWER: 1, AUTHORITY: 2, ADDITIONAL: 2

;; QUESTION SECTION:
;web1.example.net.              IN      A

;; ANSWER SECTION:
web1.example.net.      300     IN      A       10.1.2.5

;; AUTHORITY SECTION:
example.net.           300     IN      NS      ns2.example.net.
example.net.           300     IN      NS      ns1.example.net.

;; ADDITIONAL SECTION:
ns1.example.net.       300     IN      A       10.1.1.3
ns2.example.net.       300     IN      A       10.1.1.4

;; Query time: 2 msec
;; SERVER: 192.168.0.1#53(192.168.0.1)
;; WHEN: Mon Mar 19 20:48:27 2012
;; MSG SIZE  rcvd: 118
```

This is a lot of output, but there's a lot of useful information here. First let's look at the question and answer sections:

```
;; QUESTION SECTION:
;web1.example.net.              IN      A

;; ANSWER SECTION:
web1.example.net.      300     IN      A       10.1.2.5
```

The question section repeats what DNS query was sent. In this case, we asked for the A record (the traditional DNS record that maps a hostname to an IP) for web1.example.net. The answer section returns the full A record for web1.example.net including its IP address (10.1.2.5) and its TTL (Time To Live—how many seconds we can cache this reply before we should look it up again), which in this case is 300 seconds.

Along with the answer to our direct query, the DNS reply sent up some additional information:

```
;; AUTHORITY SECTION:
example.net.            300    IN    NS    ns2.example.net.
example.net.            300    IN    NS    ns1.example.net.

;; ADDITIONAL SECTION:
ns2.example.net.        300    IN    A     10.1.1.4
ns1.example.net.        300    IN    A     10.1.1.3
```

In the authority section, we get two NS records for example.net. An NS record is a special DNS record that lists which hosts are registered as name servers for a particular zone. In the authority section, we see that there are two name servers for example.net, ns2.example.net and ns1.example. net, and both of them happen to also have a TTL of 300 seconds. After the authority section is the additional section that lists extra information our DNS query gave us. In this example, it provided us with the A records for ns2.example.net and ns1.example.net, so we know both of their IP addresses. The DNS server does this so that the next time we look up records for example.net, we may already have the NS records along with their IP cached, and this saves time because we do not have to look those up again.

Finally, the dig output gives us some information about our query itself:

```
;; Query time: 2 msec
;; SERVER: 192.168.0.1#53(192.168.0.1)
;; WHEN: Mon Mar 19 20:48:27 2012
;; MSG SIZE  rcvd: 118
```

Although this output might be easy to skip over, it also provides us with some valuable information. It not only tells us when we ran the query and how long it took (which can be useful when we are diagnosing slow DNS servers), it also tells us what DNS server did the search for us. This can be handy in case we are trying to track down a problem where one DNS server has stale records and another doesn't, because we can tell which DNS server our client contacted for each request.

By default dig attempts to resolve a hostname into an IP, but you can also have dig bring back any other DNS record for a domain. To do this, just add the record type to the end of your query (i.e., NS, MX, TXT). This is particularly handy when you want to know what name servers or mail servers are configured for a particular domain:

```
$ dig example.net NS
; <<>> DiG 9.7.0-P1 <<>> example.net NS
;; global options: +cmd
;; Got answer:
;; ->>HEADER<<- opcode: QUERY, status: NOERROR, id: 38194
;; flags: qr aa rd ra; QUERY: 1, ANSWER: 2, AUTHORITY: 0, ADDITIONAL: 2

;; QUESTION SECTION:
;example.net.                     IN      NS

;; ANSWER SECTION:
example.net.            300      IN      NS      ns1.example.net.
example.net.            300      IN      NS      ns2.example.net.

;; ADDITIONAL SECTION:
ns1.example.net.        300      IN      A       10.1.1.3
ns2.example.net.        300      IN      A       10.1.1.4

;; Query time: 3 msec
;; SERVER: 192.168.0.1#53(192.168.0.1)
;; WHEN: Sat Mar 24 20:44:42 2012
;; MSG SIZE  rcvd: 98
```

You'll find this sort of dig query much more useful as we troubleshoot zone transfer issues further on in this chapter and mail server troubleshooting in Chapter 7.

Trace a DNS Query

Generally speaking, when you look up a DNS record, your machine doesn't look everything up itself; instead, you send your request to a DNS server

provided by your organization or ISP and it does all of the DNS heavy lift-
ing for you. In many cases, unless the DNS server already has the answer
cached, it usually does not already know the answer to your question, so
it has to do what is known as **recursive DNS resolution.** If we assume no
cache is involved, a recursive DNS resolver has to go through quite a few
steps before it can get your answer.

In the case of web1.example.net, first the resolver sends the request to one of
the 13 root name servers—the most important name servers on the Internet. These name servers are crucial for recursive queries, so all name servers
that are going to perform recursive queries have the root name server IP
addresses hard-coded. The root name servers don't know the address for
web1.example.net, but they do have a list of all the .net name servers, so
they reply with those along with their IP addresses. Then the resolver asks
one of the .net name servers for the address for web1.example.net. The .net
name servers don't have that information either, but they do know the list
of name servers responsible for example.net, so they reply with that, along
with their IPs. Finally, when the resolver asks one of those servers for the
address for web1.example.net, it replies back with the record (if it exists)
and the resolver finally returns back to you with your answer.

That was a lot of steps, and if you are new to DNS, sometimes it can be
hard to remember how recursive DNS resolution works, but dig provides
a nice feature in that it can perform complete, uncached, recursive DNS
requests for you and show you the complete trace for the request. You can
think about it sort of like traceroute for DNS. To enable this feature, just
add +trace to the end of your dig request:

```
$ dig web1.example.net +trace

; <<>> DiG 9.7.0-P1 <<>> web1.example.net +trace
;; global options: +cmd
;; global options: +cmd
.                  143557  IN      NS      m.root-servers.net.
.                  143557  IN      NS      a.root-servers.net.
.                  143557  IN      NS      b.root-servers.net.
.                  143557  IN      NS      c.root-servers.net.
.                  143557  IN      NS      d.root-servers.net.
.                  143557  IN      NS      e.root-servers.net.
```

```
.                         143557  IN     NS     f.root-servers.net.
.                         143557  IN     NS     g.root-servers.net.
.                         143557  IN     NS     h.root-servers.net.
.                         143557  IN     NS     i.root-servers.net.
.                         143557  IN     NS     j.root-servers.net.
.                         143557  IN     NS     k.root-servers.net.
.                         143557  IN     NS     l.root-servers.net.
;; Received 512 bytes from 192.168.0.1#53(192.168.0.1) in 3 ms

net.                      172800  IN     NS     a.gtld-servers.net.
net.                      172800  IN     NS     k.gtld-servers.net.
net.                      172800  IN     NS     b.gtld-servers.net.
net.                      172800  IN     NS     d.gtld-servers.net.
net.                      172800  IN     NS     l.gtld-servers.net.
net.                      172800  IN     NS     e.gtld-servers.net.
net.                      172800  IN     NS     f.gtld-servers.net.
net.                      172800  IN     NS     m.gtld-servers.net.
net.                      172800  IN     NS     h.gtld-servers.net.
net.                      172800  IN     NS     g.gtld-servers.net.
net.                      172800  IN     NS     j.gtld-servers.net.
net.                      172800  IN     NS     i.gtld-servers.net.
net.                      172800  IN     NS     c.gtld-servers.net.
;; Received 503 bytes from 192.33.4.12#53(c.root-servers.net) in 22 ms

example.net.              172800  IN     NS     ns2.example.net.
example.net.              172800  IN     NS     ns1.example.net.
;; Received 102 bytes from 192.12.94.30#53(e.gtld-servers.net) in 153 ms

web1.example.net.         300     IN     A      10.1.2.5
example.net.              300     IN     NS     ns2.example.net.
example.net.              300     IN     NS     ns1.example.net.
```

Above each line that begins with ;; is the output from the request sent to that server. If we look at just the lines that begin with ;;, we can see what servers were involved in the request:

```
;; Received 512 bytes from 192.168.0.1#53(192.168.0.1) in 3 ms
;; Received 503 bytes from 192.33.4.12#53(c.root-servers.net) in 22 ms
;; Received 102 bytes from 192.12.94.30#53(e.gtld-servers.net) in 153 ms
;; Received 118 bytes from 10.1.1.4#53(ns2.example.net) in 2 ms
```

The first server was 192.168.0.1, the local DNS server, which replied with the list of root name servers. The next request went to c.root-servers.net, one of the root name servers, which replied with a list of .net name servers. By the way, you might have noticed that all of the root name servers are named after a letter in the alphabet, but by default, name server replies are sent in random order. That way you can pick the first server in the list and the load gets balanced evenly. The next request in the list was sent to e.gtld-servers.net, a .net name server, which returns the list of name servers for example.net. The final request went to ns2.example.net, which replied back with the answer we were looking for.

I highly recommend trying out the +trace argument both for domains you own and for any domain you might visit frequently. The output provides an instant primer on how recursive resolution works, and if you run it for your own domain while everything is working well, you'll have a nice baseline to compare against when things go wrong.

Recursive Name Server Problems

Now that we've gone over how DNS requests generally work, we'll discuss problems in the very next link in the chain: recursive name servers. Most computers don't have a DNS server installed on them; instead, all DNS queries go to a recursive name server. On Linux machines these name servers are configured in /etc/resolv.conf. Although that DNS server might host some zones itself, as a recursive name server, it will receive DNS queries from clients and then perform recursive resolution (the steps we discussed in the tracing section) to resolve them.

When a recursive name server has a problem, all clients using that name server have a problem. Since we all rely on DNS to translate hostnames to IPs, without your recursive name server, you won't be able to look up IP addresses for your favorite websites, and unless you have IPs memorized, the Internet will, in effect, be down for you.

Because recursive DNS resolution is so important, ISPs provide their clients with more than one name server to use, and most offices and other organizations should as well. In those cases, when the first name server in your list has a problem, one of the first symptoms you might see is DNS resolution taking about 30 seconds. If you aren't directly doing

DNS lookups on the command line, this would be apparent when you try to load a new website in a browser and it lags for about 30 seconds before it loads.

If you suspect that one of your recursive DNS servers is down, confirming the suspicion is pretty straightforward. Go through the list of name servers configured for your host (listed in /etc/resolv.conf on Linux) and perform DNS client troubleshooting, as discussed at the beginning of the chapter, to see if your list of name servers are up and replying. Basically, use nslookup to attempt to resolve a few well-known and presumably stable sites like www.google.com and www.yahoo.com, only make sure to add the IP address of the name server you want to test after the query, like so:

```
$ nslookup www.google.com 10.1.1.4
Server:        10.1.1.4
Address:       10.1.1.4#53

Non-authoritative answer:
www.google.com   canonical name = www.l.google.com.
Name:    www.l.google.com
Address: 74.125.224.144
Name:    www.l.google.com
Address: 74.125.224.145
Name:    www.l.google.com
Address: 74.125.224.146
Name:    www.l.google.com
Address: 74.125.224.147
Name:    www.l.google.com
Address: 74.125.224.148
```

If you follow the steps from the DNS client troubleshooting section, you should be able to tell whether the DNS server is up and reachable or not. Once that's confirmed, and you still can't resolve sites, you might see an error like the following:

```
$ nslookup www.example.net 10.1.1.4
Server:        10.1.1.4
Address:       10.1.1.4#53

** server can't find www.example.net: REFUSED
```

The dig command provides a more direct error message in its output:

```
$ dig www.example.net 10.1.1.4

; <<>> DiG 9.7.0-P1 <<>> www.example.net @10.1.1.4
;; global options: +cmd
;; Got answer:
;; ->>HEADER<<- opcode: QUERY, status: REFUSED, id: 23822
;; flags: qr rd; QUERY: 1, ANSWER: 0, AUTHORITY: 0, ADDITIONAL: 0
;; WARNING: recursion requested but not available

;; QUESTION SECTION:
;www.example.net.          IN    A

;; Query time: 1492 msec
;; SERVER: 10.1.1.4#53(10.1.1.4)
;; WHEN: Sat Mar 24 20:15:17 2012
;; MSG SIZE  rcvd: 33
```

In both cases, what you see is that the DNS server is up and responding, however, your request was refused. In the dig output, you can see the explanation that the request was refused because recursion was not available.

What has happened here is probably the cause of a misconfiguration, especially if the name server has worked before. Many organizations restrict what hosts are allowed to perform recursive queries on them for security reasons, which you can see if you attempt to resolve a site like google.com from something like yahoo.com's name servers. It is likely that an admin changed a configuration file and accidentally disabled recursion altogether, or if recursion was limited to certain IP addresses, the admin accidentally removed the IPs.

In BIND, recursion is turned on by default but can be disabled or restricted via its configuration file. This option is configured either in the root named.conf file (usually at /etc/bind/named.conf) or in one of the other configuration files that named.conf includes, such as named.conf.local or named.conf.options on some servers. The option you want to search, called either recursion or allow-recursion, is in the options section of the file, and might look like the following:

```
options {
    allow-recursion { 10.1.1/24; };
...
};
```

In this example, recursion is allowed for the entire 10.1.1.0 subnet. You might also see something like the following:

```
acl "internal" { 127.0.0.1; 192.168.0.0/24; 10.1.0.0/16; };

options {
    allow-recursion { "internal"; };
...
};
```

Here, instead of specifying an IP address, we specified an ACL (Access Control List) called "internal" that we defined earlier in the configuration file to be a list of IP addresses. BIND allows you to do this so you can define ACLs in one place and then reference them multiple times through your config. If you see a line like the preceding one in your BIND configuration file and recursion isn't working, make sure that your client's IP address is in the list of networks that are allowed.

If, on the other hand, you see something like this,

```
options {
    recursion no;
...
};
```

then recursion has been disabled on this name server. To enable it, either remove this option so BIND will switch to its default of recursion being on, or better yet, replace it with an allow-recursion statement so BIND can restrict recursion to specific networks. In either case, once you are done, restart the BIND server to make sure the changes take.

When Updates Don't Take

As a DNS administrator, one of the more common problems you might have to troubleshoot is a change you've made to your zone files that doesn't take. Even if you aren't responsible for the DNS server, knowing how to troubleshoot update problems is a handy skill to have in your arsenal. After all, if you ask your administrator to make the change, or if you make the change via some DNS hosting service and you keep getting the old record, it can be handy to know how to figure out where the problem is.

Most DNS update problems fall into three camps: updates you don't see (yet) because of DNS caching, updates the DNS server rejects because of syntax errors, and problems due to the changes made to the master DNS server not making it to its slave hosts. This section discusses how to identify each type of problem using the same DNS troubleshooting tools we've used so far.

DNS Caching and TTL   The fact is that your average DNS record might stay the same for weeks, months, or even years. Because many DNS records are so stagnant, it doesn't make much sense for every DNS query to have to follow that same long path we covered in the tracing section of this chapter. Instead, as a DNS server does a query, it caches its results so that if you make the same request afterward, it can return an answer much more quickly.

Of course the problem with caching is, how does the DNS server you use know how long to cache results? The answer is that each DNS record contains a Time To Live, or TTL, value measured in seconds. When you perform a DNS request, the server you use checks its cache, and any records that are newer than their respective TTLs are returned to you from the cache, even if they might have changed on the host. Once the TTL of a record expires, the DNS server goes through its regular steps to resolve the IP; however, note that each DNS server it queries along the way also has a TTL of its own, and if those TTLs haven't yet expired, it will just use the IPs it has in cache. This is why you often hear the refrain, "it may take up to two days to see your change in DNS." In particular, the root and top level domain name servers have long TTLs, so when you register a new domain, it may take some time for those changes to propagate. Although your average TTL is a few hours, TTLs can range from as little as under a minute to multiple days, and depending on the kind of change, it might take quite some time for all the related caches to expire.

Although DNS caching can be quite handy, one problem for DNS administrators is that not every DNS server out there honors your TTL. In fact, some ISPs have been known to completely disregard TTLs that are too low, to help reduce the load on their DNS servers. Because of this, even though you may have a TTL of only a few minutes, a DNS change you make may take hours to show up on a DNS server that doesn't obey it.

The easiest way to see the TTL for a zone, outside of viewing it on the DNS server itself, is via the dig command:

```
$ dig web1.example.net
; <<>> DiG 9.7.0-P1 <<>> example.net
;; global options: +cmd
;; Got answer:
;; ->>HEADER<<- opcode: QUERY, status: NOERROR, id: 30750
;; flags: qr aa rd ra; QUERY: 1, ANSWER: 1, AUTHORITY: 2, ADDITIONAL: 2

;; QUESTION SECTION:
;web1.example.net.              IN      A

;; ANSWER SECTION:
web1.example.net.      300     IN      A       10.1.2.5

;; AUTHORITY SECTION:
example.net.           300     IN      NS      ns2.example.net.
example.net.           300     IN      NS      ns1.example.net.

;; ADDITIONAL SECTION:
ns1.example.net.       300     IN      A       10.1.1.3
ns2.example.net.       300     IN      A       10.1.1.4

;; Query time: 2 msec
;; SERVER: 192.168.0.1#53(192.168.0.1)
;; WHEN: Mon Mar 19 20:48:27 2012
;; MSG SIZE  rcvd: 118
```

Along with each record dig reports back, it also includes the TTL, not just for the main record you requested, but also for any additional information it may return. In this case, the TTLs for all the records happen to be 300 seconds. This tells us that if we make a change to the web1.example.net record, we can expect it to take up to 5 minutes for an ordinary DNS server to return the new record.

Of course, if you have made an update and aren't seeing it, how do you know for sure it's a caching issue and not some other problem? The best way to tell is to identify one of the official name servers for the domain (in the earlier dig output, you see it's ns2.example.net and ns1.example.net). If you aren't sure what name servers are used by a domain, just perform a dig query for the NS records:

```
$ dig example.net NS

; <<>> DiG 9.7.0-P1 <<>> example.net NS
;; global options: +cmd
;; Got answer:
;; ->>HEADER<<- opcode: QUERY, status: NOERROR, id: 38194
;; flags: qr aa rd ra; QUERY: 1, ANSWER: 2, AUTHORITY: 0, ADDITIONAL: 2

;; QUESTION SECTION:
;example.net.                 IN      NS

;; ANSWER SECTION:
example.net.          300    IN      NS      ns1.example.net.
example.net.          300    IN      NS      ns2.example.net.

;; ADDITIONAL SECTION:
ns1.example.net.      300    IN      A       10.1.1.3
ns2.example.net.      300    IN      A       10.1.1.4

;; Query time: 3 msec
;; SERVER: 192.168.0.1#53(192.168.0.1)
;; WHEN: Sat Mar 24 20:44:42 2012
;; MSG SIZE  rcvd: 98
```

Once you have the list of name servers, choose one and query it directly:

```
$ dig web1.example.net @10.1.1.4
```

When you query a name server directly, you bypass any caching from your local DNS server and get the current up-to-date record, so if the IP you get from your direct query is still the old IP, you know that the change hasn't propagated to that name server. At that point, query the rest of the name servers in the list directly and see if any of them have the correct record. If you find that none of the DNS servers have the update, you may have a syntax error in your zone file. If some DNS servers have the update and others don't, you might have a zone transfer issue.

If you do find that the name servers do have the correct record but your local DNS server has the old record cached, you have a few recourses. The simplest recourse is to just wait until the local cache expires. Ideally, if you know in advance that you need to make a DNS change and your TTL is long, many DNS administrators lower the TTL a few days before the change so that all DNS servers out there have a chance to pull down the new shorter TTL. Then, once the change goes through, they increase the TTL back to its old value.

If you can't wait until the local cache expires, you can also flush your respective DNS caches. The first cache to flush would be the cache located on your operating system. Yes, even your OS will cache DNS requests so it doesn't have to query your name server every time a record needs to be resolved. On Linux the nscd daemon (if it's installed) handles this caching, so to flush its cache just type

```
$ sudo /etc/init.d/nsdc restart
```

If you are on a Windows system, you can open a command prompt and type

```
ipconfig /flushdns
```

On a Mac, you would open a terminal and type

```
lookupd -flushcache
```

or the following, depending on your version of Mac OSX:

```
dscacheutil -flushcache
```

If it's your recursive DNS server that holds the cache, you will need to have administrative access to it to flush its cache. To flush the DNS cache of a BIND name server, you simply restart the service. On Red Hat-based systems this might be

```
$ sudo /etc/init.d/named restart
```

On Debian-based systems the service might be called bind or bind9 instead of named. If you don't have the ability to restart your recursive name server, the only alternative is to temporarily replace the name server configured for your system with one that doesn't have the old record cached, or, you could hard-code the IP in your /etc/hosts file, but that is a short-sighted fix that I don't recommend.

Zone Syntax Errors If you have made a change to a DNS record and notice that the update hasn't made it to any of the name servers for that zone, a likely cause is a syntax error in the zone file. When you make a change to a zone file and then reload BIND, if it notices a syntax error in the file, it will simply disregard any changes to that particular zone file and stick to the records it has. Unless you pay attention to the log files, you may not even realize it happened. If you updated a zone, reloaded the BIND service, and the name server still reports the old record, check /var/log/syslog or /var/log/messages on your system for error messages from BIND.

Here's an example error message as a result of a syntax error:

```
Mar 27 21:07:26 ns1 named[25967]: /etc/bind/db.example.net:20: #ns2.example.net: bad owner
➥name (check-names)
Mar 27 21:07:26 ns1 named[25967]: zone example.net/IN: loading from master file /etc/bind/
➥db.example.net failed: bad owner name (check-names)
Mar 27 21:07:26 snowball named[25967]: zone example.net/IN: not loaded due to errors.
```

In this case, the first line in the error message is kind enough to tell me that the error is in line 20 of /etc/bind/db.example.net. What happened here is a classic mistake: Almost all configuration files support using # to comment out a line except BIND, which uses a semicolon. Instead of using the semicolon to comment out a line in the zone file, the administrator accidentally used # and BIND rejected the zone.

Zone Transfer Issues The last problem we'll discuss that can cause a DNS change to not take is due to zone transfer issues. In your average DNS infrastructure, one DNS server is treated as the master for a particular zone and the rest are configured as slaves. Any changes are made to the master and then are pushed out to any slaves that are configured. Zone transfer problems can be tricky to detect immediately because your master name server will report the new record; however, any queries to one or more slaves may report the old record. As a result, different clients may see different IP addresses at different times.

The fastest way to identify a zone transfer issue is perform a direct DNS query using a tool like dig against all of the name servers configured for a zone. If you see that some name servers have the change and others don't, wait a minute or two and try again to see if the changes possibly just took some time to propagate. If after a few minutes the changes still aren't transferred, then the next step is to identify the master DNS server and confirm it has the right records. The master DNS server is configured in a special record called the Start of Authority, or SOA, record. This record lists what is considered to be the authoritative DNS server for the zone and, like with other dig requests for specific record types, simply query the domain and add SOA to the end of the query:

```
$ dig example.net SOA

; <<>> DiG 9.7.0-P1 <<>> example.net SOA
;; global options: +cmd
;; Got answer:
;; ->>HEADER<<- opcode: QUERY, status: NOERROR, id: 62609
;; flags: qr aa rd ra; QUERY: 1, ANSWER: 1, AUTHORITY: 2, ADDITIONAL: 2

;; QUESTION SECTION:
;example.net.                   IN      SOA

;; ANSWER SECTION:
example.net.            300     IN      SOA     ns1.example.net. admin.example.net.
  ➥2011062300 10800 2000 604800 7200
```

```
;; AUTHORITY SECTION:

example.net.            300    IN    NS    ns2.example.net.

example.net.            300    IN    NS    ns1.example.net.


;; ADDITIONAL SECTION:

ns1.example.net.    300    IN    A     10.1.1.3

ns2.example.net.    300    IN    A     10.1.1.4


;; Query time: 35 msec

;; SERVER: 192.168.0.1#53(192.168.0.1)

;; WHEN: Tue Mar 27 21:18:46 2012

;; MSG SIZE  rcvd: 143
```

In this output, we're particularly interested in this line:

```
;; ANSWER SECTION:

example.net.            300    IN    SOA    ns1.example.net. admin.example.net.
  ↪2011062300 10800 2000 604800 7200
```

Here you see that the authoritative DNS server is ns1.example.net. The next record after that, admin.example.net, isn't another name server but instead is actually the email address to the administrative contact for this domain. The first period is intended to be replaced by an @, so in this case the administrative contact is admin@example.net.

Once you know which name server is authoritative for a zone, that's the server that should be configured as the master. If we suspect there is a zone transfer issue, the next step is to log in to the master DNS server directly and check its configuration.

The way that zone transfers work in BIND is that any time a record is updated on the master, BIND scans the zone for the NS records and notifies each of those name servers that there is an update. If BIND is configured with an extra list of name servers to notify in addition to name servers configured in the zone, it notifies those as well. The slave name servers are configured to know who their master or masters are and will disregard this notification if it doesn't come from the list of masters. Along with the notification the master will send a serial number configured in the zone file that is supposed to be incremented each time the zone changes. If the serial number on the master is larger than the serial number on the slave, the slave will request either a full or partial zone transfer so it gets the updates. That zone transfer request goes back to the master and, provided it comes from an IP address that it allows to have zone transfers (by default all of the configured name servers for the zone are allowed), the master will start the zone transfer. A problem with any of the above steps can cause an update to fail, so we'll discuss how to identify each problem.

Once you make a change to a zone and reload BIND, the master should show that the change was detected and that a notify was sent:

```
Mar 27 21:47:16 ns1 named[25967]: zone example.net/IN: loaded serial 2012032700
Mar 27 21:47:16 ns1 named[25967]: zone example.net/IN: sending notifies (serial 2012032700)
```

If you don't see evidence in the logs that notifies were sent, then it's time to troubleshoot the configuration on your master. First, use commands like this to see if the named process is even running:

```
$ ps -ef | grep named
```

If it is not, start the service. You may also have to resort to restarting the BIND daemon if it didn't reload properly. Finally, check your BIND named.conf and the rest of the zone configuration files, and confirm that this particular zone is configured to be a master and not a slave on this server.

One of the most common reasons a zone transfer fails is simply that the serial number wasn't updated. When you reload BIND on the master you might see an error in the logs like the following:

```
Mar 27 21:09:52 ns1 named[25967]: zone example.net/IN: zone serial (2012011301) unchanged.
  ↪zone may fail to transfer to slaves.
Mar 27 21:09:52 ns1 named[25967]: zone example.net/IN: loaded serial 2012011301
Mar 27 21:09:52 ns1 named[25967]: zone example.net/IN: sending notifies (serial 2012011301)
```

In this case, you are being warned that the serial number did not change even though the zone did. If you see a message like this, simply re-edit your zone file and make sure the serial number is incremented (many DNS administrators use the YYYYMMDD format followed by two more numbers to allow them to update a zone up to 100 times in a day while also letting them easily see the last time the zone was updated). If the notify went out and the serial number is larger than what is on the slaves, you should see entries like the following in the log file on your master:

```
Mar 27 21:47:16 ns1 named[25967]: client 10.1.1.4#38239: transfer of 'example.net/IN':
➥AXFR-style IXFR started
Mar 27 21:47:16 ns1 named[25967]: client 10.1.1.4#38239: transfer of 'example.net/IN':
➥AXFR-style IXFR ended
```

Here you see that the transfer for the zone that changed was started by the client 10.1.1.4 and then ended. You should see an entry like this for each name server configured for this zone, and if you don't, while you are on the master, make sure that all of the name servers that need updates are either configured in the zone itself with their own NS entry or in your named.conf file in the also-notify directive (if configured).

If the log files and configuration on the master seem correct but you don't see that a zone transfer was initiated, the next step is to go to a slave name server. You should be able to see entries in the /var/log/syslog or /var/log/ messages file on the slave name server that show it received a notify that a zone has changed:

```
Mar 27 21:58:44 ns2 named[22774]: client 10.1.1.3#50946: view external: received notify for
➥zone 'example.net'
Mar 27 21:58:44 ns2 named[22774]: zone example.net/IN/external: Transfer started.
Mar 27 21:58:44 ns2 named[22774]: transfer of 'example.net/IN' from 10.1.1.3#53: connected
➥using 10.1.1.3#38239
Mar 27 21:58:44 ns2 named[22774]: zone example.net/IN/external: transferred serial
➥2012032700
Mar 27 21:58:44 ns2 named[22774]: transfer of 'example.net/IN' from 10.1.1.3#53: end of
➥transfer
```

These log entries show a complete zone transfer process that was successful; however, you might see a log entry like the following:

```
Mar 27 21:58:45 ns2 named[22774]: zone example.net/IN/external: refused notify from non-
  ➥master: 10.1.1.7#35615
```

Here the slave received a notify from a server (in this case 10.1.1.7) that it does not have configured as its master, so it rejected it. In this case, if the IP is a valid IP for the master, you will need to look into your BIND configuration for this zone on this slave and make sure that it is configured as a slave and that the IP of the master is configured as one of the master IPs.

You might, on the other hand, see a log entry like the following:

```
Mar 27 22:09:00 ns2 named[22774]: client 10.1.1.3#42895: view external: received notify for
  ➥zone 'example.net'
Mar 27 22:09:00 ns2 named[22774]: zone example.net/IN/external: notify from 10.1.1.3#42895:
  ➥zone is up to date
```

In this case the notification was sent to the slave; however, the serial number was not larger than the serial number on the slave, so it didn't bother updating. An administrator might accidentally set a very high serial number on the master (like using the date as a serial number but accidentally setting the year wrong) but doesn't realize it and sends out an update. Then when the next administrator comes around, they fix the error by setting the serial number to the current date again, but the slaves refuse to accept the update. When this happens, the fix is to log in to the slave and view the local cached zone files it has for that zone. Where it stores these files is something that is configured in BIND, but common locations include the /var/cache/bind, /etc/bind, and /var/lib/bind directories. When you open this file you should see all of the records for your zone much like they are configured in the master, and at the top of the file you can see what the serial number is set to. If the serial number is too high, the easiest solution is to simply delete or move this file, then restart BIND on the slave. The BIND service should then request a zone transfer from the master and get up to date.

## CHAPTER 7

Why Didn't My Email
Go Through?
Tracing Email Problems

ALONG WITH DNS, EMAIL is one of the oldest and most widely used services on the Internet. Unlike DNS, most people use email directly and frequently and are aware when there's a problem. No matter what role you have on a DevOps team, if you are responsible for email service in any capacity, whether as the administrator in charge of the email server, the go-to tech guy at an office, a developer adding email support to an application, or just a regular email user yourself, eventually you will have to answer one of the following questions:

- I sent an email but the recipient didn't get it, what happened?
- Someone sent me an email but I didn't get it, what happened?

This chapter will talk about how to troubleshoot email, specifically how to solve problems related to sending and receiving email using SMTP (Sendmail Transfer Protocol). This sort of troubleshooting is related, but different from troubleshooting mailbox retrieval over protocols like POP and IMAP. Even though there are many mail servers out there, troubleshooting ordinary problems with email delivery is the same on all servers. Since IMAP and POP troubleshooting can vary widely depending on their servers, and since the techniques are quite different, this chapter will just stick to SMTP. If you are interested in troubleshooting IMAP or POP problems, I recommend looking at documentation specifically geared for your IMAP or POP server. By the end of the chapter, you should have the techniques and tools to track down (as much as is possible) why an email wasn't delivered.

Trace an Email Request

Before we dive into how to troubleshoot specific email problems, it's useful to first understand just what happens when you send an email. If you are able to mentally trace an email from your computer to your recipient along with each stop along the way, when there is a problem you can follow the path your email should have taken through each step and better figure out which step failed.

Email systems are set up in many different ways, and if you get email through a large email provider, their systems might be quite complex. The fact is, even with a complex mail provider, the general way that email gets sent is still pretty much the same, so when you trace an email, you'll want to base it on a simple, average case.

For this example, let's assume that we want to send an email from our corporate email account, kyle@example.net, using some desktop email client like Thunderbird or Outlook, and let's assume this is all hosted on a mail server called mail.example.net controlled by the company. We want to send the email to our personal Gmail account, you@gmail.com, and since we don't know the inner workings of Google's mail servers, we will treat the mail servers like a normal mail server on the Internet.

First, when we click Send, our email client communicates with the outbound mail service it is configured to use over SMTP. In this case, it would likely be a local mail server inside the office and may even be the same machine we use to retrieve email over IMAP (but it doesn't have to be). This outbound mail server (here called mail.example.net) should be configured to allow us to relay email through it. Mail servers that allow anyone to relay mail through them are called open relays, and ever since spammers started finding and using open relays to send spam, most mail servers restrict who can relay mail through them. Some servers restrict this based on IP address whereas others require the client to authenticate with a login and password first.

Once mail.example.net accepts my email, it puts it in the mail spool along with any other email that needs to be delivered. When it is ready to send the message, it scans the FROM address for the destination domain (in this case gmail.com). Then it performs a DNS query to find out all of the MX records for gmail.com (similar to dig gmail.com MX) and gets back results like the following:

```
5 gmail-smtp-in.1.google.com.
10 alt1.gmail-smtp-in.1.google.com.
20 alt2.gmail-smtp-in.1.google.com.
30 alt3.gmail-smtp-in.1.google.com.
40 alt4.gmail-smtp-in.1.google.com.
```

In this case, there are five different mail servers to choose from and each mail server has a priority assigned to it. The mail.example.net server will pick the remote mail server with the lowest priority (in this case that would be gmail-smtp-in.l.google.com, which has a priority of 5). Once it has selected the mail server to contact, it initiates an SMTP connection with it over port 25.

If for some reason the first server doesn't respond, mail.example.net will pick from the remaining list of gmail.com mail servers based on what has the lowest priority. If none of the mail servers are available, mail.example. net will requeue the email and try again later. Most email servers will continue to try to deliver an email for a few days before giving up. When the mail server does give up, it will send you a bounce email letting you know that the message was unable to be delivered. This is an important point because if all the remote mail servers for a remote domain are unavailable (or your mail server has network problems of its own and is unable to reach them), it may take days before the email bounces. Generally this is a good thing because you want your mail server to keep trying to deliver messages, but because so many users are accustomed to emails being delivered almost instantaneously, a lag of even an hour might be a problem.

Let's assume that the first gmail.com mail server is up. When mail.example. net makes its SMTP connection, it tells gmail.com who it is, who the email is from, and who the email is to. Since the gmail.com mail server isn't an open relay, it will only accept email that is destined to be delivered on it (email sent to gmail.com and any other domains it is responsible for). Although mail.example.net is connected to it, at a minimum it examines the domain the email is addressed to and makes sure it is for a domain it accepts. The mail server may also check who the email is addressed to and confirm it's a valid account. If either of these checks fails, it will reject the message with an error code and mail.example.net will send us a bounce email.

Spam is a big concern for mail administrators, so the gmail.com mail server might perform some extra checks while mail.example.net is connected. For instance, it might check to see if mail.example.net is listed in one of the many spam blackhole lists as a spammer. It might also perform a number of other checks against the mail server to make sure it is valid. If any of these initial spam checks fail, it will reject the message with an error code and we will get a bounce email.

If the email makes it through all of these checks, the gmail.com mail server will send a success response to mail.example.net, disconnect from it, and then add the email to the queue for delivery. Of course at this point most mail servers will also run additional spam filtering on the message based on the body, but if it does flag the message as spam, it won't send a bounce message or otherwise notify mail.example.net at all. From the perspective of mail.example.net the mail was delivered successfully.

If the mail server that accepted the message is not the primary mail server with the lowest priority, it will add the email to the spool and attempt to deliver it to the primary mail server for the next few days. After that point, if it is unable to deliver it, it will remove the email and send a bounce message. Once the email is successfully on the primary mail server, it will either deliver the email to a local mailbox if it also acts as the POP and IMAP server, or it will be configured to forward the messages to a different mail server where it will ultimately end up in your inbox.

Understand Email Headers

Now that we've traced an email through the system, the headers in an email make a lot more sense. By default when you view email, a lot of the headers are left out and you are left with To, From, Subject, and the body of the message. There are extra headers at the top of the email that provide valuable troubleshooting data specifically related to how the email got from the sender to the recipient. Although most mail clients hide these headers by default, there should be an option to view the hidden headers in your mail client. For instance, in Gmail, the option appears in a drop-down menu when you view the message and is named Show Original.

As an example, we could send a test email from kyle@example.net to a Gmail account, you@gmail.com, to simulate the email tracing example mentioned earlier. In a normal email client, here is what you might see:

```
Date: Wed, 11 Apr 2012 19:55:43 -0700
From: Kyle Rankin <kyle@example.net>
To: you@gmail.com
Subject: Test Subject

Test Body
```

Here are the full contents of the email:

```
Delivered-To: you@gmail.com
Received: by 10.182.250.51 with SMTP id yz19csp53077obc;
        Wed, 11 Apr 2012 19:55:45 -0700 (PDT)
Received: by 10.42.179.196 with SMTP id br4mr523278icb.42.1334199345073;
        Wed, 11 Apr 2012 19:55:45 -0700 (PDT)
Return-Path: <greenfly@example.net>
Received: from mail.example.net (mail.example.net. [64.142.5.5])
        by mx.google.com with ESMTPS id s4si19571254igb.48.2012.04.11.19.55.44
        (version=TLSv1/SSLv3 cipher=OTHER);
        Wed, 11 Apr 2012 19:55:44 -0700 (PDT)
Received-SPF: pass (google.com: best guess record for domain of greenfly@example.net
  ↪designates 64.142.5.5 as permitted sender) client-ip=64.142.5.5;
Authentication-Results: mx.google.com; spf=pass (google.com: best guess record for domain
  ↪of greenfly@example.net designates 64.142.5.5 as permitted sender) smtp.mail=greenfly@
  ↪example.net
Received: by mail.example.net (Postfix, from userid 1000)
id 7F566254A3; Wed, 11 Apr 2012 19:55:43 -0700 (PDT)
Date: Wed, 11 Apr 2012 19:55:43 -0700
From: Kyle Rankin <kyle@example.net>
To: you@gmail.com
Subject: Test Subject
Message-ID: <20120412025543.GD23360@example.net>
MIME-Version: 1.0
Content-Type: text/plain; charset=us-ascii
Content-Disposition: inline
User-Agent: Mutt/1.5.20 (2009-06-14)

Test Body
```

As you can see, a lot of extra information is in the email that you normally
don't see, and the bulk of the extra headers are like a postmark on an
envelope. Each mail server the email goes through to get to its destination,
starting with the initial mail server, leaves a Received header with a date
stamp and information about the message. The next mail server in the list
adds its header to the top of the message, and so on, so that the header
you see at the very top of the message is actually the last mail server that
ultimately received the message:

```
Received: by 10.182.250.51 with SMTP id yz19csp53077obc;
        Wed, 11 Apr 2012 19:55:45 -0700 (PDT)
```

So if you want to trace the path the email took, you want to look at the Received headers in reverse order. To help illustrate this, let's repaste the headers but in reverse order so you can see the path the email took. First, here is the email as it was accepted by the mail.example.net mail server:

```
Received: by mail.example.net (Postfix, from userid 1000)
          id 7F566254A3; Wed, 11 Apr 2012 19:55:43 -0700 (PDT)
```

Next we see that a Gmail mail server, mx.google.com, received the message from mail.example.net, and that it ran it through an initial spam check to see if mail.example.net was an acceptable host for the email to come from. These headers prove that the email left mail.example.net and was accepted by Google's mail servers. Also note that each Received header assigns its own ID to the email—these IDs can be useful later on as they should correspond to IDs used in the mail logs on the mail servers:

```
Received: from mail.example.net (mail.example.net. [64.142.5.5])
          by mx.google.com with ESMTPS id s4si19571254igb.48.2012.04.11.19.55.44
          (version=TLSv1/SSLv3 cipher=OTHER);
          Wed, 11 Apr 2012 19:55:44 -0700 (PDT)
Received-SPF: pass (google.com: best guess record for domain of greenfly@example.net
     ⮑designates 64.142.5.5 as permitted sender) client-ip=64.142.5.5;
Authentication-Results: mx.google.com; spf=pass (google.com: best guess record for domain
     ⮑of greenfly@example.net designates 64.142.5.5 as permitted sender) smtp.mail=greenfly@
     ⮑example.net
```

From this point on, the headers we see give a glimpse into the internal structure of Google's mail infrastructure as it lists two more servers the email is sent to, the final one being the destination:

```
Received: by 10.42.179.196 with SMTP id br4mr523278icb.42.1334199345073;
          Wed, 11 Apr 2012 19:55:45 -0700 (PDT)
Received: by 10.182.250.51 with SMTP id yz19csp53077obc;
          Wed, 11 Apr 2012 19:55:45 -0700 (PDT)
```

Problems Sending Email

So now that you are familiar with the path a successful email takes, it should be a bit simpler to track down problems sending email. This section assumes that at least you have control over the settings of your email client, and at most, you have control of the outbound mail server your client uses to send out email. Essentially, the goal is to make sure the outbound mail server accepts your mail and is able to communicate with the destination mail server that then accepts the email for initial delivery. Later this chapter will cover how to troubleshoot problems receiving email.

When you tell your email client to send mail, it is configured to talk to a specific outbound mail server that might be entirely different from the machine it talks to when it receives email. This mail server is not required to be listed in DNS with an MX record, although that might help it pass more spam tests on the remote mail server. Essentially the outbound mail server just needs to be listening on some incoming port (usually TCP port 25, or possibly port 465 for SMTP over SSL, although that's more rare), it needs to be configured to allow certain hosts (hopefully not all) to relay email through it, and it needs to be able to communicate with other mail servers on the Internet.

A few main issues can prevent you from sending email. First, your client can't communicate with the outbound mail server. Second, the mail server won't allow you to relay through it. Third, the mail server can't communicate with the destination mail server or the mail server can communicate with the remote mail server, but the email is rejected for a number of reasons.

Client Can't Communicate with the Outbound Mail Server

Your email won't get very far if you can't communicate with your outbound mail server. If this is the problem, your mail client will probably alert you with a message that says the outbound mail server is unavailable. The first step is to simply attempt to send the email again to see if it was just a one-time hiccup. If you still get an error, it's time to perform some basic network troubleshooting against this host.

Chapter 5 discusses how to perform network troubleshooting when you can't communicate with a remote host. Before you go much further in this chapter, make sure your client can communicate with other hosts on your network. If it can't, go to Chapter 5 to figure out why. If you can talk to other hosts on your network, then you can skip ahead in that chapter to specific troubleshooting against the mail server.

Let's assume that the mail server is our standard mail.example.net that we've used for other examples, and that it has an internal IP of 10.1.1.20; you can just replace this host and IP with the server you have configured in your mail client as an outbound mail server. If you are reasonably sure the computer can communicate on the network, then skip ahead in Chapter 5 to the Is DNS Working? section and follow its directions to confirm you can resolve mail.example.net into its IP address. Then follow the next steps in Chapter 5 in the Can I Route to the Remote Host? section to confirm you can route to mail.example.net. If all of that is successful, then it's finally time to perform some SMTP-specific steps.

The next step is to confirm whether your host can communicate with port 25 on mail.example.net (or whatever port you have configured to use for the outbound mail server in your client). To do this, adapt the steps from the Is the Remote Port Open? section through the Firewall Rules section of Chapter 5 to SMTP. Those sections are aimed at web server troubleshooting, not SMTP, but with a few substitutions, the same steps can apply to SMTP. Where the sections talk about port 80, substitute port 25; everywhere they talk about Apache, substitute it with your email server software (such as Postfix); and everywhere they talk about web1, substitute the hostname of your outbound mail server.

Once you have gone through all of the network troubleshooting steps and have confirmed your host can communicate with the outbound mail server, the next step is to confirm that you can successfully complete an SMTP transaction with the outbound mail server by using one of the best troubleshooting techniques: sending test emails with telnet.

Send a Test Email with Telnet   With the advent of secure, encrypted remote shell programs like SSH, telnet is often relegated to the retirement home of command-line utilities, but telnet can still be a quite useful tool when you want to test network communications by hand.

First, tell telnet to connect to port 25 on your mail server:

```
$ telnet mail.example.net 25
Trying 10.1.1.20...
Connected to mail.example.net.
Escape character is '^]'.
220 mail.example.net ESMTP Postfix
```

Now that we are connected, we can start typing raw SMTP commands. The first command is HELO and lets the server know what domain you are coming from. It will then respond with its name:

```
HELO kylepc.example.net
250 mail.example.net
```

Next, we use the MAIL FROM: command to tell the mail server the FROM email address to use. What's interesting here (and fun for pranks) is that generally you can post any FROM address you want here. If the mail server accepts it, it will reply with 250 Ok:

```
MAIL FROM: <kyle@example.net>
250 Ok
```

Note that we surrounded the email with <>. Although some email servers are lenient about this rule, some mail servers are strict and will return a syntax error if the email address isn't surrounded by <>. Once we get this 250 Ok response, we are halfway through with testing the mail server. Now we send the RCPT TO: command so the server knows who the email is for. In this case, we'll send the email to you@gmail.com:

```
RCPT TO: <you@gmail.com>
250 Ok
```

If you were communicating with a destination mail server here, and the account you specified in the RCPT TO: field was invalid, the mail server would return an error code. Once you get to this point, you can be pretty well assured that the mail server has accepted the message and will attempt to deliver it. Type DATA and press Enter. The mail server will respond with instructions to end your email body with an empty line containing a single dot. You can also add any additional headers to your email in the body—the Subject: header is one of the most popular. When you're done with the message, type a period on a line by itself:

```
DATA
354 End data with <CR><LF>.<CR><LF>
Subject: Testing email 1
Hi,

I'm just testing email service
.
250 Ok: queued as 12BDBE6FEE9
```

I like putting something unique like an ascending number in the Subject for test emails. In the course of troubleshooting, you might find that you send multiple emails, and it's nice to be able to identify each test email and the order in which it was sent. The server will respond with 250 Ok: followed by the queue ID. If you have a login on the server itself, you can use this ID as a keyword to trace the email through the mail logs. When you're finished with your email session, type quit to exit:

```
quit
221 Bye
Connection closed by foreign host.
```

Email Error Codes   You might have noticed in the telnet test that the server responded to each of our requests with a code, usually 250. Each request made to the mail server gets a reply code so the client knows whether it was successful. The most common code is 250, which means that the previous command was completed. Essentially, any code that starts with a 2 denotes a success, so for instance, when we typed quit, we received the code 221, which means that the remote server is going to close the connection.

Codes that start with a 3 denote commands that are accepted, however, they require additional information to complete. A good example of this is when we issued the DATA command: We got a 354 code back, which means the server is waiting for us to input the data followed by the single period on its own line.

Codes that start with a 4 are for temporary errors and mean that the sender should send their request again—usually from the beginning. You might see errors like this if the remote mail server is unusually busy, its disk is full, or if there is some other temporary local error on the system. When a properly configured mail server gets this error code, it should retry the connection at a later date. For instance, some mail administrators set up what's known as **greylisting** to reduce spam. Greylisting works on the premise that most spam mail servers have so much spam to send that if they are told to try again later, they won't bother. The first time a mail server with greylisting enabled gets a connection from a remote mail server, it replies back with the error code 450 and the instructions to try back in a few minutes.

Error codes that start with 5 denote a permanent error; they can range from syntax (501) or other command errors that all start with 50, to codes that start with 55 and denote more common errors such as the mailbox being unavailable (550), and the mailbox being full (552), to the mailbox name not being allowed (553), and a general transaction failure (554).

Outbound Mail Server Won't Allow Relay

Open relays are mail servers that are configured to accept incoming email from any host and relay it to any other mail server. In the days before spam, open relays were relatively common, but nowadays any email server on the open Internet that relays mail for any other host gets flagged by spam blackhole lists and quickly finds itself blocked by other mail servers.

Today an outbound mail server used to relay mail should either be firewalled off from incoming SMTP traffic from the Internet, or better, set up with a restricted list of IPs or subnets it will accept mail from. Even better than that, some mail servers use authentication, such as SMTP auth, so that they only relay mail from clients with the right username and password. If you find that your mail client is able to connect to the mail server but it gets an error message back stating relay access is denied, your problem is likely with one of the just-mentioned relay safeguards.

If the mail server uses SMTP authentication, then the next troubleshooting step is to verify the account—your password probably expired or otherwise changed. If the mail server doesn't use SMTP authentication, the next step is to look at the configuration of the mail server and confirm that relaying is enabled and that your client's IP address is on the list of approved IPs and networks. For instance, on postfix this is set via the smtpd_recipient_restrictions configuration option, which you could check with the postconf command:

```
$ postconf smtpd_recipient_restrictions
smtpd_recipient_restrictions = permit_mynetworks, permit_sasl_authenticated,
    ↪reject_unauth_destination
```

If you are using postfix, you may just have a subset of these options enabled (this server supports authentication), but likely you will have permit_mynetworks enabled. This option allows relaying for any networks set in the mynetworks option, which you can also check with the postconf command:

```
$ postconf mynetworks
mynetworks = 127.0.0.0/8, 192.168.0.0/24
```

Here you can see the mail server accepts email from localhost (127.0.0.0/8) and from the 192.168.0.x network.

Outbound Mail Server Can't Communicate with the Destination

If you can successfully queue an email with your outbound mail server but it still doesn't seem to get delivered, the next step is to test the communication between the outbound mail server itself and the destination mail server. If you have access to the outbound mail server, log in and view the mail logs (on a Linux system often at /var/log/mail.log or /var/log/maillog) and see if you can locate one of your messages in the log. If you performed the telnet email test, then you were given an email queue ID once you submitted the body of the email in a response something like this:

```
250 Ok: queued as 12BDBE6FEE9
```

The fastest way to find information about this email is to use the grep command and search for the email ID:

```
$ grep 12BDBE6FEE9 /var/log/mail.log
Apr 17 20:16:50 mail postfix/smtpd[25545]: 12BDBE6FEE9: client=kylepc.example.net[75.101.46.232]
Apr 17 20:17:03 mail postfix/cleanup[25564]: 12BDBE6FEE9: message-id=<>
Apr 17 20:17:03 mail postfix/qmgr[10784]: 12BDBE6FEE9: from=<kyle@example.net>, size=252,
   ↪nrcpt=1 (queue active)
Apr 17 20:17:05 mail postfix/smtp[25586]: 12BDBE6FEE9: to=<you@gmail.com>, relay=gmail-smtp-
   ↪in.1.google.com[173.194.79.27]:25, delay=21, delays=19/0.06/0.89/0.68, dsn=2.0.0,
   ↪status=sent (250 2.0.0 OK 1334719025 vs4si1566804pbc.307)
Apr 17 20:17:05 mail postfix/qmgr[10784]: 12BDBE6FEE9: removed
```

In this log example, you can see who the email was from (kyle@example.net), who the email was to (you@gmail.com), who the destination mail server was (gmail-smtp-in.1.google.com), and that the destination mail server accepted the message with a 250 success code (250 2.0.0 OK). If you see a log entry like this for the email, then the destination mail server did accept and spool the email you sent. This is proof that there is nothing wrong with your outbound mail server, but that the problem is on the remote mail server's end (possibly the email ended up in a spam folder). If there was some sort of problem communicating with the remote mail server, you would see error codes in place of the 250 success code in these logs, and these would give you more detail on the nature of the problem.

At this phase, a number of things could prevent you from delivering email to the destination mail server. For one, your mail server could have been rejected for anti-spam measures. This might happen if a machine inside the network gets hacked or gets a virus and starts sending out spam through your mail server. If this is the case, you should see some sort of error code starting with 5, and often you will also see a brief explanation of what spam rule the mail server is breaking along with a URL for even more details.

If you were blocked because of spam, solving the problem usually involves contacting the administrator of an SBL (Spam Blackhole List) via a web form and requesting that they remove your mail server from the list. Otherwise, typically the URL you're pointed to gives good instructions on how to unblock your mail server and correct whatever triggered the problem in the first place.

If, on the other hand, you see an error stating that your mail server can't communicate with the remote mail server, you might also notice multiple attempts as the mail server attempts to deliver the email every so often. At this phase, what you will want to do is repeat the steps in the Client Can't Communicate with the Outbound Mail Server section you performed earlier to test network connectivity between your client machine and the outbound mail server, only this time, perform the tests *from* the outbound mail server and perform the tests *against* the destination mail server.

If you aren't sure about what mail server you should communicate with for the destination mail server, you can either use the same hostname your outbound mail server tried to contact in your mail logs, or you can perform a dig query to find out all of the mail servers for a particular domain. For instance, to find out the mail servers for the gmail.com domain, you would type

```
$ dig gmail.com MX +short
5 gmail-smtp-in.l.google.com.
10 alt1.gmail-smtp-in.l.google.com.
20 alt2.gmail-smtp-in.l.google.com.
30 alt3.gmail-smtp-in.l.google.com.
40 alt4.gmail-smtp-in.l.google.com.
```

Start your network troubleshooting back in Chapter 5, only substitute any references to web servers and port 80 with port 25. Pick the destination server that has the lowest priority (in this example that is gmail-smtp-in.l.google.com with a priority of 5). Then, for example, when you get to the nmap phase of the network troubleshooting steps, run nmap from the outbound mail server and list gmail-smtp-in.l.google.com as the host to scan:

```
$ nmap -p 25 gmail-smtp-in.l.google.com

Starting Nmap 5.00 ( http://nmap.org ) at 2012-04-17 20:31 PDT
Note: Host seems down. If it is really up, but blocking our ping probes, try -PN
Nmap done: 1 IP address (0 hosts up) scanned in 3.11 seconds
```

Notice that at first you didn't get a proper response back from nmap. This is because the remote machine might have been blocking ping probes. In this case, you follow nmap's helpful instructions and add -PN to the command:

```
$ nmap -p 25 -PN gmail-smtp-in.1.google.com

Starting Nmap 5.00 ( http://nmap.org ) at 2012-04-17 20:32 PDT
Interesting ports on pb-in-f27.1e100.net (173.194.79.27):
PORT    STATE SERVICE
25/tcp open  smtp

Nmap done: 1 IP address (1 host up) scanned in 0.14 seconds
```

Here you can see that the remote SMTP port is open. If it were closed, either your mail server would be blocked from communicating with this machine (more likely all remote servers) over port 25, or the remote mail server would be down. To test both theories, try the same nmap command against a mail server for a completely different domain (like yahoo.com, for instance) and also against the next mail server in the list for gmail.com and see if either of their ports are open.

If you discover both remote mail servers are closed on port 25, it's more likely that your firewall or your ISP's firewall is blocking outbound port 25 traffic than it is that multiple enterprise mail servers for different companies are down at the same time. If, on the other hand, only Gmail's mail servers are unavailable, then it's possible they are just suffering an outage right now, in which case the best thing to do is just let your mail server continue to try to deliver the email. It shouldn't bounce the message until it has tried to deliver it for at least a few days.

If your mail server has been firewalled off from sending emails, or you are waiting for a remote mail server to come back online, your mail spool might start to fill up with email destined for that domain. The mailq command run from the outbound mail server will give you information about the current state of the mail queue:

```
$ mailq
Mail queue is empty
```

In this case, the mail queue is empty, which ideally is what you want to see. Otherwise, you will see how many messages are currently waiting in the queue along with their queue ID and who they are addressed to.

Once mail service is restored, the mail server will attempt to deliver all of those spooled messages, but not at once. Instead, it will slowly spool them so as not to risk overloading itself. If, for some reason, you can't wait and need those messages delivered immediately, your mail server should provide some sort of flush command that will let you immediately spool all email for delivery. Note that you will probably need to be root to run this command. For instance, with postfix the command is

```
$ sudo postqueue flush
```

Problems Receiving Email

It can be tricky to know when you have a problem receiving email for a particular domain unless you sent the email yourself from a different account. You won't know an email didn't reach you if you didn't know it was sent. Usually this sort of problem is realized when an email sent to your domain bounces, or more likely, someone sends you or someone in your organization an important email, expecting real-time responses. When they don't get responses, they call or contact the recipient directly with a "Hey, did you get my email?" When this happens, as the trouble-shooter, you need to be able to demonstrate a few things: First, your mail system is successfully receiving other emails, and second, you can or can't locate the email conversation for that specific email in the logs.

This section will walk through a simple system where a single incoming mail server receives mail. In most cases, you will want at least two mail servers, one acting as a secondary in case the primary ever goes down. If you have a setup like that, you will need to perform these troubleshooting steps on all of the incoming mail servers you have configured.

One easy way to test that your mail system is functioning, particularly if it is a busy system, is to log in to it and view the mail logs in real time with tail -f /var/log/mail.log (or /var/log/maillog on some systems). If you have an active mail server, you should be able to see emails coming in for other users. If you see other email activity, then the mail server is functioning in general and the next step is to pore through the logs. On the other hand, if you have a mostly inactive mail server or you aren't seeing new log entries, the best next step is to perform the same steps as a remote mail server, only manually. Before you do that, though, if you truly aren't getting any incoming email and you suspect you should, you may want to perform a quick dig query and confirm that your incoming mail server is listed as one of the mail servers for your domain and that its IP address is correct:

```
$ dig example.net MX
```

Now that you have confirmed that your mail server is listed in DNS, it's time to simulate a remote mail server. To do this, get onto a machine, ideally one that's outside of your network, and perform the telnet email test mentioned earlier in the chapter, only this time, connect to your incoming mail server (whatever mail server has the highest priority MX record), and address the email to you or the user that is complaining about an email not going through. If your mail server accepts your telnet test and the email shows up in the recipient's mailbox, you can be relatively sure general incoming mail is being accepted for that user.

Telnet Test Can't Connect

There are a few ways the telnet test can fail, however. For one, you might discover you can't connect to your mail server from the outside at all; in this case, it's time to log in to the incoming mail server and make sure the mail server software is running. For instance, on a system running postfix, you might type

```
$ sudo /etc/init.d/postfix status
 * postfix is running
```

If you are running sendmail or exim, you can replace postfix with the name of your server's init script. Alternatively, you can also simply check whether any postfix processes are running with the ps command. This has the advantage that you can run it without root permissions:

```
$ ps -ef | grep postfix
postfix  10784 16923  0 Jan13 ?       00:02:44 qmgr -l -t fifo -u -c
postfix  10820 16923  0 Jan13 ?       00:00:39 tlsmgr -l -t unix -u -c
root     16923     1  0 2011 ?        00:24:15 /usr/lib/postfix/master
postfix  18320 16923  0 20:23 ?       00:00:00 pickup -l -t fifo -u -c
postfix  20304 16923  0 20:36 ?       00:00:00 anvil -l -t unix -u
root     20426 12533  0 20:38 pts/2   00:00:00 grep postfix
```

If the process isn't running, then the solution is simple: Start the process. Otherwise, the next step is to confirm that the mail server is listening on port 25:

```
$ sudo netstat -lnp | grep :25
tcp        0      0 0.0.0.0:25          0.0.0.0:*            LISTEN      16923/master
```

Here you can see that process 16923 (named master, the main postfix process) is listening on port 25 on all interfaces (0.0.0.0). If you saw that it was listening on 127.0.0.1 instead, for instance, you would know that the mail server only listens for email on localhost, and if you want it to accept email from the outside, you'll need to reconfigure it. Otherwise, if you see that no processes are listening on port 25 but your mail server is running, you have some sort of configuration problem you need to address.

Finally, if you do see that the mail server is running and listening on the correct port, attempt to do another telnet test from the host itself by telnetting to 127.0.0.1 port 25 and confirm that you can connect. If you can, then try again, only this time connect from a server on the same subnet. If both attempts are successful, then there's a good chance the problem is caused by some firewall or routing issue that is preventing your server from being contacted from the outside.

Telnet Can Connect, but the Message Is Rejected

Once telnet can connect to the mail server and you send your test email, you should be able to see any delivery problems that a remote mail server would see. For instance, if the user's mailbox is full, the disk is full in general, or there's some other server problem, you should get an error message when you try to send your test email that tells you where to investigate next.

If, on the other hand, the message is accepted, confirm that it ends up in the recipient's mailbox. If the email doesn't make it in the mailbox, then you have some problem between your mail server and your POP/IMAP server (or, if it's on the same machine, a problem handing off incoming email to your local mailboxes). If the email does make it in the mailbox, then you can be reasonably sure the mail server is functioning correctly at the present time, and it's time to dig through the logs to find out what happened to the original message that wasn't delivered.

Pore Through the Mail Logs

If your mail server seems to be accepting other email fine, you now need to see if you can find evidence that the remote mail server attempted to connect to your incoming mail server and deliver the email. If you are responding to a user complaint, see if you can find out a range of time when the email was supposed to have been sent and the FROM email address. Both of those facts will help you when you dig through your mail logs.

For instance, if the user's email address is jan@example.net and Jan tells you that Fred (fred.smith@gmail.com) emailed her around 8:00 a.m. this morning but she hasn't gotten the email yet, that should be enough information to go on to get started. With that information the first thing you would do is open your current /var/log/mail.log and with a program like less, and skip through until you got to logs from around 8:00 a.m. You're not necessarily trying to find Jan's message specifically here, but just performing a sanity check to see whether other messages were delivered around that time period. The fact is, even if the mail system were down at that time, the message would have either been queued in a secondary mail server, or once the mail server came back online the message should have gotten delivered shortly afterward.

After you're convinced the mail server was functioning around that time, next you'd attempt to filter out all of Jan's incoming email out of the mail log for today into a different file so it can be a bit easier to pore through:

```
$ sudo egrep 'to=.*jan@example.net' /var/log/mail.log > /tmp/jans_incoming_emails
```

If Jan had told you that the email was sent a few days ago instead of today, you would replace /var/log/mail.log with the archived mail log that has entries for that day. In either case, now you can open /tmp/jans_incoming_emails with a text editor and see first, if Jan got any other messages, and second, what kind of messages she got around 8:00 a.m.. If you wanted to get fancy, you could run another grep command that filtered out messages outside of a time range, but just to be safe look at messages from an hour before and an hour after 8:00 a.m. at least. In the process of going through this file if you find any emails that fit that time period, you'll want to view the full message transaction, so you need to pull out the message ID. For instance, the log entry you were interested in might look like this:

```
Apr 19 08:05:06 incoming postfix/local[13089]: 62337254A2: to=<jan@example.net>,
➥relay=local, delay=4.7, delays=0.4/0.03/0/4.3, dsn=2.0.0, status=sent (delivered to
➥command: /usr/bin/procmail -t)
```

You could pull out the message ID 62337254A2 from that line and then go back to the main /var/log/mail.log and grep the entire message transaction:

```
$ sudo grep 62337254A2 /var/log/mail.log
Apr 19 08:05:02 incoming postfix/smtpd[13058]: 62337254A2: client=unknown[23.19.244.190]
Apr 19 08:05:02 incoming postfix/cleanup[13081]: 62337254A2: message-id=<Z3J1ZW5mbH1AZ3J1ZW
➥5mbHkubmV0882@quickclickdeals.info>
Apr 19 08:05:02 incoming postfix/qmgr[10784]: 62337254A2: from=<contest@quickclickdeals.
➥info>, size=11382, nrcpt=1 (queue active)
Apr 19 08:05:06 incoming postfix/local[13089]: 62337254A2: to=<jan@example.net>,
➥relay=local, delay=4.7, delays=0.4/0.03/0/4.3, dsn=2.0.0, status=sent (delivered to
➥command: /usr/bin/procmail -t)
Apr 19 08:05:06 incoming postfix/qmgr[10784]: 62337254A2: removed
```

In this case, this is the wrong message (and likely spam) since the FROM header is not fred.smith@gmail.com.

An alternate approach while looking through the mail logs is that instead of looking for email to Jan, you could look for email from Fred. After all, what if he misspelled Jan's email address somehow, the email bounced, but Fred didn't notice. To do that, just pull out any messages from his address instead:

```
$ sudo egrep 'from=.*fred.smith@gmail.com' /var/log/mail.log > /tmp/freds_incoming_emails
```

Then you can see if there are any message IDs from Fred and go back to the main log to see if he ever made an attempt to begin with. Finally, you might even simply grep for any messages referencing gmail.com at all:

```
$ sudo grep 'gmail.com' /var/log/mail.log > /tmp/gmail_all_emails
```

From this log you could see if there were any emails from that domain at all during the general time period Jan laid out. If at this point you still don't see anything in the logs, feel confident going back to Jan and saying you simply don't see the email attempt in the logs and to have the sender send it again. Ultimately you might even end up working with the administrator in charge of the remote site and compare log entries. It all might depend on how important these emails are. Even if the problem doesn't appear to be on your end, you might still be on the hook to track down the root cause of the problem, even if it's another administrator's fault.

## CHAPTER 8

Is the Website Down? Tracking Down Web Server Problems

ALTHOUGH DNS AND EMAIL are important Internet services that we inter-act with on a daily basis, web services tend to get much more of our direct attention. You may or may not immediately notice when someone else's email server or DNS server is down, but if your favorite website is down, you will know almost instantly. Plus, many applications have moved from being run on local systems to being run on a web server accessed from your web browser instead. With so much riding on the health of web servers, you are likely to be responsible for one in some way, and it's more important than ever to be able to troubleshoot web server problems.

Everyone in a DevOps organization is likely to troubleshoot web server problems at some point in time. On the QA side, many of the automated testing and build tools you use on a daily basis operate via a web front-end, not to mention in this day and age that it's likely you might be perform-ing some level of automated testing on a web-based application. When a web server is unresponsive, you'll want the tools to trace down why. On the developer end, it's more likely than ever that you will be developing software that has at least some level of web front-end, if it is not already entirely run from the web. Plus, in a DevOps team, developers often take on more of a role in web server configuration than on traditional teams, and they hold more responsibility over troubleshooting sluggish or unavailable web servers. Of course, if you are a sysadmin, it's quite likely you will be responsible for at least some web servers in your environment, and you will likely be one of the first people to answer that dreadful ques-tion: "Is the website down?"

In a chapter about web server troubleshooting, it is quite easy to get bogged down in troubleshooting steps for particular web frameworks, content management systems, plugins, or blogging platforms that would turn this chapter into a full book in its own right and still not necessar-ily help you with your custom web app. Instead, this chapter will provide general, basic troubleshooting steps you can apply to gauge the health of two popular web servers: Apache and Nginx. The idea here is to give you overall tools and techniques you can apply to most web server problems so that no matter what specific web server software you run, when there is a problem, you can get closer to narrowing it down.

Is the Server Running?

One of the first web server problems to troubleshoot is a web server that's completely unavailable. This is such a common set of troubleshooting steps that it was already used as the primary example throughout Chapter 5 to diagnose networking issues. After all, one of the first questions you want to answer when you can't reach a web server is whether the problem is on your end or the remote end. For a complete set of network troubleshooting steps, I highly recommend you go through Chapter 5 first; however, this chapter assumes that the problem is not on the network, so it will repeat some of the web-server specific troubleshooting steps from Chapter 5. In this example, the server is named web1 and has an IP address of 10.1.2.5, so be sure to change your commands to match the hostname and IP for your web server.

Is the Remote Port Open?

So you can route to the machine, but you can't access the web server on port 80. The next test is to see whether the port is even open. There are a number of different ways to do this. For one, you could try telnet:

```
$ telnet 10.1.2.5 80
Trying 10.1.2.5...
telnet: Unable to connect to remote host: Connection refused
```

If you see Connection refused, then either the port is down (likely Apache isn't running on the remote host or isn't listening on that port) or the firewall is blocking your access. If telnet can connect, then, well, you don't have a networking problem at all. If the web service is up but just isn't working the way you expect it to, you need to investigate your Apache configuration on the web server.

Instead of telnet, I prefer to use nmap to test ports because it can often detect firewalls. If nmap isn't installed, use your package manager to install the nmap package. To test web1, you would type the following:

```
$ nmap -p 80 10.1.2.5
Starting Nmap 4.62 ( http://nmap.org ) at 2009-02-05 18:49 PST
```

```
Interesting ports on web1 (10.1.2.5):
PORT STATE SERVICE
80/tcp filtered http
```

Aha! nmap is smart enough that it can often tell the difference between a closed port that is truly closed and a closed port behind a firewall. Now normally when a port is actually down, nmap will report it as closed. Here it reported it as filtered. What this tells us is that there is some firewall in the way that is dropping the packets to the floor. This means you need to investigate any firewall rules on the gateway (10.1.1.1) and on web1 itself to see if port 80 is being blocked.

Test the Remote Host Locally

At this point, we have either been able to narrow the problem down to a network issue or we believe the problem is on the host itself. If we think the problem is on the host itself, we can do a few things to test whether port 80 is available.

Test for Listening Ports   Once you are satisfied that the problem is not on you network, you should log in to the web server and test whether port 80 is listening. The netstat -lnp command will list all ports that are listening along with the process that has the port open. You could just run that and parse through the output for anything that is listening on port 80, or you could use grep to see only the things that are listening on port 80:

```
$ sudo netstat -lnp | grep :80
tcp 0 0 0.0.0.0:80 0.0.0.0:* LISTEN 919/apache
```

The first column tells you what protocol the port is using. The second and third columns are the receive and send queues (both set to 0 here). The column you want to pay attention to is the fourth column, as it lists the local address on which the host is listening. Here the 0.0.0.0:80 tells us that the host is listening on all of its IPs for port 80 traffic. If Apache were listening only on the server's Ethernet address, you would see a specific IP like 10.1.2.5:80 here.

The final column tells you which process has the port open. Here you can see that Apache is running and listening. If you do not see this in your netstat output, you need to start your Apache server.

Firewall Rules If the process is running and listening on port 80, it's possible that the server has some sort of firewall in place. Use the iptables command to list all of your firewall rules. If your firewall is disabled, your output would look like this:

```
$ sudo /sbin/iptables -L
Chain INPUT (policy ACCEPT)
target     prot opt source            destination

Chain FORWARD (policy ACCEPT)
target     prot opt source            destination

Chain OUTPUT (policy ACCEPT)
target     prot opt source            destination
```

Notice that in this output, the default policy is set to ACCEPT. It's possible, though, that your firewall is set to drop all packets by default, even if it doesn't list any rules. If this is the case, you would see output more like the following:

```
$ sudo /sbin/iptables -L
Chain INPUT (policy DROP)
target     prot opt source            destination

Chain FORWARD (policy DROP)
target     prot opt source            destination

Chain OUTPUT (policy DROP)
target     prot opt source            destination
```

On the other hand, if you have a firewall rule that blocks port 80, it might look like this:

```
$ sudo /sbin/iptables -L -n
Chain INPUT (policy ACCEPT)
```

```
target      prot opt source                destination
REJECT      tcp  --  0.0.0.0/0             0.0.0.0/0                tcp dpt:80
reject-with icmp-port-unreachable

Chain FORWARD (policy ACCEPT)
target      prot opt source                destination

Chain OUTPUT (policy ACCEPT)
target      prot opt source                destination
```

Clearly, in the latter case, you need to modify the firewall rules to allow port 80 traffic from the host.

Test a Web Server from the Command Line

Once you are convinced that the web server is actually listening on the correct port, the next troubleshooting step is to confirm that the web server actually responds to requests. Although it's true that you could use a web browser to test this, if you know how to troubleshoot a web server with a command-line tool like curl or telnet, you can test your web server from just about any host (and more importantly, over an ssh connection). After all, most servers don't have a GUI web browser installed, and you may not even be able to guarantee that command-line web browsers like curl, links, or w3m are installed, but telnet almost certainly will be. Because of this, this chapter will show you how to test your web server both with curl and with telnet as a fallback.

Test Web Servers with Curl

Curl is a relatively straightforward command-line tool that can speak the HTTP and HTTPS protocols, among others. If you check out its man page (by typing man curl on the command line), you'll see that it supports all sorts of different options. In fact, a number of command-line tools used to interface with web APIs use curl exclusively. Curl has an advantage over raw telnet for web server troubleshooting in that it takes care of the HTTP protocol for you and makes things like testing authentication, posting data, using SSL, and other functions we take for granted in a GUI web browser much easier. With telnet, we will be typing in HTTP commands directly.

Since we just want to test basic web server functionality, we don't necessarily need to get into any of curl's more sophisticated command-line options. In fact, testing a web server from curl can be as simple as typing curl and then the URL to load:

```
$ curl http://www.example.net
<html><body><h1>It works!</h1>
<p>This is the default web page for this server.</p>
<p>The web server software is running but no content has been added, yet.</p>
</body></html>
```

In this example, you can see the default web page created by an Apache web server. If for some reason the web server were unreachable, you would see something like

```
$ curl http://www.example.net
curl: (7) couldn't connect to host
```

By default, curl will just output the contents of the web page you requested, but often when you troubleshoot web servers you'd like to get extra data, such as the HTTP status code (more on that later), how long the request took, how much data was transferred, and so on. Curl offers a -w option that lets you pull additional data about the request and display it on the screen. So, for instance, if you wanted to see the HTTP status code for a request, you could type

```
$ curl -w "%{http_code}\n" http://www.example.net
<html><body><h1>It works!</h1>
<p>This is the default web page for this server.</p>
<p>The web server software is running but no content has been added, yet.</p>
</body></html>
200
```

The extra information gets posted at the end of the request. In this case, the HTTP status code is 200, which is what we want. The curl man page (type man curl) lists a number of extra options for the -w argument that you can chain together in your output. Here's an example of how you might use that to get the status code, how long the request took, the size of the data downloaded, and the content type:

```
$ curl -w "%{http_code} %{time_total} %{size_download} \
%{content_type}\n" http://www.example.net
<html><body><h1>It works!</h1>
<p>This is the default web page for this server.</p>
<p>The web server software is running but no content has been added, yet.</p>
</body></html>
200 0.004 177 text/html
```

Test Web Servers with Telnet

Although curl is a handy and simple tool for testing web servers on the command line, sometimes you might need to test a web server from a host that doesn't have curl installed, or you may just need to see lower-level HTTP calls. In either case, that's where telnet comes in. Just about any Linux system should have telnet installed and, as long as you know some basic HTTP, you can get a lot of valuable diagnostic data from a web server.

To start, run telnet with the host you want to connect to as an argument, followed by port 80, or whatever port your web server is listening on:

```
$ telnet www.example.net 80
Trying 10.1.2.5...
Connected to www.example.net.
Escape character is '^]'.
```

If for some reason you can't connect, then you will need to go back to the initial network troubleshooting section in this chapter. Once you are connected, you will type in some basic HTTP:

```
GET / HTTP/1.1
host: www.example.net
```

This example uses a basic GET request (GET /) that requests the default index page for the site followed by what HTTP protocol you're using (HTTP/1.1). If you wanted to test the /admin/inventory.cgi page, for instance, you would say GET /admin/inventory.cgi HTTP/1.1. Then you press Enter and follow up with a host: and the name of the host you want to connect to (what would be directly after the http:// in a URL). This host parameter is important since web servers often serve many virtual hosts on the same machine, so if you don't specify which host you want, you may not get the web pages you expect.

Once you finish the host: line, hit Enter and you should get the complete response from the server:

```
HTTP/1.1 200 OK
Date: Thu, 28 Jun 2012 03:56:32 GMT
Server: Apache/2.2.14 (Ubuntu)
Last-Modified: Mon, 24 May 2010 21:33:10 GMT
ETag: "38111c-b1-4875dc9938880"
Accept-Ranges: bytes
Content-Length: 177
Vary: Accept-Encoding
Content-Type: text/html
X-Pad: avoid browser bug

<html><body><h1>It works!</h1>
<p>This is the default web page for this server.</p>
<p>The web server software is running but no content has been added, yet.</p>
</body></html>
```

Once you are done with your request, hit Ctrl-] to quit telnet. By default, you will get a lot more troubleshooting data from telnet than with curl. In this example, you can see the HTTP status code (200 OK), the date of the request along with the last date the page was modified, the web server and version, and other data that you normally don't see in a web browser. Of course, the downside is that if you want to do anything much more sophisticated than a simple GET request, you had better brush up on your HTTP or switch back to curl, which can more easily handle redirects and other tricky setups.

HTTP Status Codes

When you are troubleshooting web server issues, the HTTP status code the web server returns with each request is invaluable. In the earlier examples, the web server returned the status code 200, which is the standard code you will see when everything is working—200 OK means the request has succeeded. There are a number of other status codes, each in their own numerical class; so, for instance, every status code that starts with 2 denotes a success and every code that starts with a 4 denotes a client error. This section talks about each of the status code classes and highlights some of the more common codes you might run into.

1xx Informational Codes

Status codes that start with 1 denote some sort of informational response. This status code range is for HTTP/1.1 and shouldn't be sent to HTTP/1.0 clients. Here are the main two responses you will see in this class:

※ **100 Continue**
This tells the client to continue with the rest of its request.

※ **101 Switching Protocols**
This indicates that the server will switch to an updated HTTP version in response to a client request to do so.

2xx Successful Codes

A status code that starts with 2 denotes a successful request. Ideally, if you are troubleshooting a web server, this is the kind of response you want to see. The most common of these status codes is 200 OK, which indicates a successful request. Here are some of the status codes you may see:

※ **200 OK**
The request was successful.

※ **201 Created**
Your request was successful and resulted in a new resource being created.

※ **202 Accepted**
Your request was accepted for processing; however, it may not have yet been processed.

▧   203 Non Authoritative Information

The information returned to you is not from the original source but may be from a third party or be a subset of the original information.

▧   204 No Content

The request was successful but the response results in no content.

▧   205 Reset Content

The client should reset the document view.

▧   206 Partial Content

The server fulfilled the partial GET request.

3xx Redirection Codes

When the status code starts with 3, it denotes some sort of redirection message from the server to the client. Administrators often use this sort of response when they have moved content from one URL to another, to move you from one domain to another, or even to redirect you to use HTTPS instead of HTTP. Here are some common status codes in this family:

▧   300 Multiple Choices

The reply from the server will contain multiple resources the client can choose to redirect to.

▧   301 Moved Permanently

This code is used when a resource will never again be available at the previous URI and has been moved to the new resource. Administrators use this code when they want to indicate that a client should point all future requests to the new URI.

▧   302 Found

Unlike the 301 status, this code denotes a resource that is only temporarily being redirected. In the future, the client should still use the original URI.

▧   303 See Other

This is commonly a response to a POST request, where the response can be obtained via a GET request to a different URI.

- **304 Not Modified**

  This response is used when the client sends a GET request conditional on the document being modified. This response lets the client know that the document has not changed.

- **305 Use Proxy**

  The server will provide a proxy in its response URI that must be followed to access the requested data.

- **306 Unused**

  Status code is not yet used.

- **307 Temporary Redirect**

  This is similar to a 302 code and is used when the resource the client is requesting can be found under a different URI temporarily, but in the future, the client should use the original URI.

4xx Client Error Codes

When you are troubleshooting server problems, you are likely to run into some error codes that start with 4. This status code family deals with errors the server believes are on the client side. The most common of these errors is 404, which is returned when a client requests a page that doesn't exist. Here are some common error codes in this class:

- **400 Bad Request**

  This code is used in response to bad syntax on the client side.

- **401 Unauthorized**

  This request requires authentication from the user, so the client should repeat the request with proper authentication.

- **403 Forbidden**

  Unlike a 401, this request is not allowed from the user and the client should not attempt to repeat the request with authentication. This error code is often indicative of permissions errors.

- **404 Not Found**

  The server couldn't find the page the client requested. This error code often comes up when the user had a typo in their request, when the request is for a page that has moved without a redirection put in place, or when the file used to exist but has been deleted.

▨ **408 Request Timeout**
The client took too long to produce a request. You may see this when you are experimenting with web server troubleshooting over telnet.

▨ **410 Gone**
Unlike a 3xx redirection request, this code is used when the resource used to exist but is now forever gone.

5xx Server Error Codes

Like 4xx status codes, 5xx status codes deal with errors, only in this case the error is likely on the server side. If you are the web server administrator and you see these kinds of error codes, you will want to dig into your web server error logs for more information on the causes of the errors. Here are some example codes from this class:

▨ **500 Internal Server Error**
The server received some internal error when it was processing the request. You may see this when you have a bug in a CGI or PHP script that causes the file to error out when it is run.

▨ **501 Not Implemented**
The server doesn't support the feature the client is requesting.

▨ **502 Bad Gateway**
The error shows up when the server is configured as a gateway or proxy device and it received an invalid response when contacting its upstream server.

▨ **503 Service Unavailable**
The server is temporarily unavailable to serve the client's request, often due to the server being overloaded or to some sort of maintenance being performed on the server.

▨ **504 Gateway Timeout**
The server did not receive a response in time from some upstream server it needed to fulfill the request. The upstream server could be

HTTP, but it could also result from a timeout in an upstream FTP, LDAP, or even DNS server.

※ **505 HTTP Version Not Supported**
Pretty self-explanatory; this error code is used when the server does not support the HTTP version the client requests.

Parse Web Server Logs

One of the primary ways you will troubleshoot web server problems is via the logs. Each request that goes to a web server gets logged in a standard format that may look a bit odd at first, but each line packs a lot of useful information for troubleshooting. Both Apache and Nginx store their logs in custom directories under /var/log/apache2 (or apache or httpd depending on your distribution) and /var/log/nginx, respectively. Both web servers default to similar log formats and both store request logs under access.log and errors under errors.log. Beyond that, though, most administrators configure their servers so that each site (virtual host) they serve has its own log, thus the access log might end up being quite empty whereas your www.example.org.log ends up containing most of your data.

To demonstrate the sorts of information you can get from web server logs, let's take a curl command used earlier in the chapter and look at the corresponding log:

```
$ curl -w "%{http_code}\n" http://www.example.net
<html><body><h1>It works!</h1>
<p>This is the default web page for this server.</p>
<p>The web server software is running but no content has been added, yet.</p>
</body></html>
200

10.1.2.3 - - [04/Jul/2012:12:08:05 -0700] "GET / HTTP/1.1" 200 303 "-" "curl/7.19.7
  ↪(x86_64-pc-linux-gnu) libcurl/7.19.7 OpenSSL/0.9.8k zlib/1.2.3.3 libidn/1.15"
```

Log entries are split up into a number of different fields, and where a field has no data or isn't applicable, it is replaced with a -. In this example, even without knowing much about the log format, we can make a few assumptions. First, the request came from the IP 10.1.2.3. Second, we can identify a date stamp for the request. After that, we can see the exact HTTP request the server processed (GET / HTTP/1.1) and the following 200 in the log corresponds to the HTTP return code. Finally, at the end of the log is the User-Agent string the client passed to the server; in this case, it identifies the client as curl.

NOTE If you are a vi user like me, you probably use it to open just about any text file including log files. Unfortunately, vi likes to store a complete copy of any text file it opens into temp space (sometimes /tmp, other times in the user's home directory). Although this practice is fine for small text files, web server logs can grow to be gigabytes in size. I can't tell you how many times I went to troubleshoot a web server that ran out of disk space only to find someone had opened up a multi-gigabyte web server log file and filled up the /tmp directory. Since we don't want to edit the web logs anyway—we just want to view them—use a command-line pager tool like less to view log files instead of vi.

Each web server allows you to customize your log output so you can get even more information about each request, but the default log format configured in Apache configuration files looks something like this:

```
LogFormat "%h %l %u %t \"%r\" %>s %0 \"%{Referer}i\" \"%{User-Agent}i\"" combined
```

Each of the symbols preceded by % represents some value to store in the logs. The complete list of these options is in the Apache documentation, but here is the description of each of these format strings:

- **%h**

  The remote host (hostname or IP)

- **%l**

  The remote logname (usually returns - unless IdentCheck is on)

- **%u**

  The remote user (if the page required authentication, otherwise returns -)

- **%t**

  The time the request was received

※ **%r**

The first line of the request

※ **%s**

The status code

※ **%0**

The bytes sent, including headers

※ **%{Header}i**

The contents of the specified header in the request

Since most web server logs are in a standard format, a lot of different tools can parse and display data from the logs. This software is useful for getting statistics and trends; however, when you are troubleshooting, often you just want to pull out data for a specific IP, or a specific URI. For this, command-line tools like grep and perl are still among the best tools, simply because they are most likely to be present on just about any web server you log into.

There are plenty of examples online of one-liners to pull data from web logs, but here are a few base examples you can build from. First is a simple grep command that will pull out all of the logs from a specific source IP. In this example, we'll look for all log entries from the host 10.1.2.3:

```
$ egrep '^10.1.2.3 ' /var/log/apache2/access.log
. . .
10.1.2.3 - - [04/Jul/2012:12:08:05 -0700] "GET / HTTP/1.1" 200 303 "-" "curl/7.19.7
 ➥(x86_64-pc-linux-gnu) libcurl/7.19.7 OpenSSL/0.9.8k zlib/1.2.3.3 libidn/1.15"
```

Alternatively, if you wanted to know just how many requests you received from that IP, you could pipe the content to wc -l, which will count the number of lines in the output:

```
$ egrep '^10.1.2.3 ' /var/log/apache2/access.log | wc -l
37
```

Of course, if your log file contains logs from multiple days, you may only be interested in the logs from a particular day:

```
$ egrep '^10.1.2.3.*04\/Jul\/2012' /var/log/apache2/access.log
```

or a particular hour in that day:

```
$ egrep '^10.1.2.3.*04\/Jul\/2012:12' /var/log/apache2/access.log
```

Using perl, you can pull even more interesting statistics from Apache logs. For instance, you may have noticed extra load on your web server today, and you'd like to know if any of that load is coming from a particular host. This perl one-liner acts like the earlier demonstrated egrep command in that it pulls out the IP and a specific date from the logs; but it goes a step further and keeps a tally of each IP it finds. Ultimately it outputs the complete list of IPs and their tally:

```
$ perl -e 'while(<>){ if( m|(^\d+\.\d+\.\d+\.\d+).*?04/Jul/2012| ){ $v{$1}++; } }
➥foreach( keys %v ){ print "$v{$_}\t$_\n"; }' /var/log/apache2/access.log | sort -n
. . .
213   27.171.3.72
217   64.2.73.9
2040  10.2.1.3
```

Here you can see that the same internal IP address (10.2.1.3) has created about ten times the number of requests of any other IP in the logs. If you were investigating a high load problem and saw this, you would pull all of the log entries coming from 10.2.1.3 and see what that internal server is doing.

In case you find that one-liner hard to parse, here's the same command in a regular file:

```
#!/usr/bin/perl

while(<>){
    if(m|(^\d+\.\d+\.\d+\.\d+).*?04/Jul/2012|){
        $v{$1}++;
    }
}

foreach( keys %v ){
    print "$v{$_}\t$_\n";
}
```

You may be tempted when first setting up a web server to enable DNS resolution for your logs. After all, wouldn't it be handy if you could automatically see what domain each visitor is coming from? It's a common mistake to enable this option when tweaking your log settings. When your server gets hit with a lot of traffic, everything slows down prematurely (or your DNS server load spikes). What's happening is that every request that comes in requires a DNS request to go out to resolve the IP into a hostname. With too many requests, you build up a backlog the server can't keep up with. The moral of the story is that if you want to resolve IPs in your web server logs into hostnames for troubleshooting, do that after the fact—-keep your web server nice and fast.

Get Web Server Statistics

Although there's a fair amount of web server troubleshooting you can perform outside of the server itself, ultimately you will get in a situation where you want to know this type of information: How many web server processes are currently serving requests? How many web server processes are idle? What are the busy processes doing right now? To pull data like this, you can enable a special server status page that gives you all sorts of useful server statistics.

Both Apache and Nginx provide a server status page. In the case of Apache, it requires that you enable a built-in module named status. How modules are enabled varies depending on your distribution; for example, on an Ubuntu server, you would type a2enmod status. On other distributions you may need to browse through the Apache configuration files and look for a commented-out section that loads the status module; it may look something like this:

```
LoadModule status_module /usr/lib/apache2/modules/mod_status.so
```

After the module is loaded on Ubuntu systems, the server-status page is already configured for use by localhost. On other systems you may need to add configuration like the following to your Apache configuration:

```
ExtendedStatus On
<IfModule mod_status.c>
#
# Allow server status reports generated by mod_status,
```

```
# with the URL of http://servername/server-status
# Uncomment and change the ".example.com" to allow
# access from other hosts.
#
<Location /server-status>
    SetHandler server-status
    Order deny,allow
    Deny from all
    Allow from localhost ip6-localhost
#    Allow from .example.com
</Location>

</IfModule>
```

Note that in this configuration example, we have really locked down who can access the page by saying deny from all hosts and only allow from local-host. This is a safe default because you generally don't want the world to be able to view this kind of debugging information. As you can see in the commented-out example, you can add additional Allow from statements to add IPs or hostnames that are allowed to view the page.

For Nginx, you would add a configuration like the following to your existing Nginx config. In this example, Nginx will only listen on localhost, but you could change this to allow other machines on your local network:

```
server {
    listen 127.0.0.1:80;

    location /nginx_status {
        stub_status on;
        access_log off;
        allow 127.0.0.1;
        deny all;
    }
}
```

Once you have your configuration set and have reloaded the web server, if you have allowed some remote IPs to view the page, open up a web browser and access /server-status on your web server. For instance, if your web server was located at www.example.net, you would load http://www.example.net/server-status and see a page like the one shown in Figure 8-1.

Apache Server Status for localhost

Server Version: Apache/2.2.14 (Ubuntu) PHP/5.3.2-1ubuntu4.15 with Suhosin-Patch
Server Built: Mar 5 2012 16:42:17

Current Time: Wednesday, 04-Jul-2012 15:23:44 PDT
Restart Time: Monday, 16-Apr-2012 22:52:21 PDT
Parent Server Generation: 16
Server uptime: 78 days 16 hours 31 minutes 23 seconds
Total accesses: 2342053 - Total Traffic: 253.6 GB
CPU Usage: u4855.07 s362.04 cu9.39 cs0 - .0769% CPU load
.344 requests/sec - 39.1 kB/second - 113.5 kB/request
2 requests currently being processed, 18 idle workers

```
. . W . _____ . _ . _ K ___ . . . . _ . _ . _ . . . . . . . . . . . . . . . . . . . .
. . . . . . . . . . . . . . _ . . . . . . . . . . . . . . . . . . . . . . . . . . . . . . . .
. . . . . . . . . . . . . . . . . . . . . . . . . . . . . . . . . . . . . . . . . . . . . . .
. . . . . . . . . . . . . . . . . . . . . . . . . . . . . . . . . . . . . . . . . . . . . . .
. . . . . . . . . . . . . . . . . . . . . . . . . . . . . . . . . . . . . . . . . . . . . . .
. . . . . . . . . . . . .
```

Scoreboard Key:
"_" Waiting for Connection, "S" Starting up, "R" Reading Request,
"W" Sending Reply, "K" Keepalive (read), "D" DNS Lookup,
"C" Closing connection, "L" Logging, "G" Gracefully finishing,
"I" Idle cleanup of worker, "." Open slot with no current process

Srv	PID	Acc	M	CPU	SS	Req	Conn	Child	Slot	Client	VHost	Request
0-16	-	0/0/58177	.	71.25	15053	0	0.0	0.00	6057.78	127.0.0.1	www.example.net.example. OPTIONS * HTTP/1.0	
1-16	-	0/0/51964	.	0.01	15049	1	0.0	0.00	4732.86	127.0.0.1	www.example.net.example. OPTIONS * HTTP/1.0	

Figure 8-1 Standard Apache status page

At the top of the status page, you will see general statistics about the web server including what version of Apache it is running and data about its uptime, overall traffic, and how many requests it is serving per second. Below that is a scoreboard that gives a nice at-a-glance overview of how busy your web server is, and below that is a table that provides data on the last request that each process served.

Although all of this data is useful in different troubleshooting circumstances, the scoreboard is particularly handy to quickly gauge the health of a server. Each spot in the scoreboard corresponds to a particular web server process, and the character that is used for that process gives you information about what that process is doing:

※   _
    Waiting for a connection

※   S
    Starting up

※   R
    Reading the request

- **W**

  Sending a reply

- **K**

  Staying open as a keepalive process so it can send multiple files

- **D**

  Performing DNS lookup

- **C**

  Closing connection

- **L**

  Logging

- **G**

  Gracefully finishing

- **I**

  Performing idle cleanup of worker

- **.**

  Open slot with no current process

Figure 8-1 shows a fairly idle web server with only one process in a K (keepalive) state and one process in a W (sending reply) state. If you are curious about what each of those processes were doing last, just scroll down the page to the table and find the process of the correct number in the scoreboard. So, for instance, the W process would be found as server 2-16. It's not apparent in the screenshot, but that process was actually the response to the request for the server-status page itself. You will also notice a few _ (waiting for connection) processes in the scoreboard, which correspond to the number of processes Apache is configured to always have running to respond to new requests. The rest of the scoreboard is full of ., which symbolize slots where new process could go—basically the MaxClients setting (the maximum number of processes Apache will spawn).

What you will notice as you refresh this page is that the objects in the scoreboard should change during each request. This scoreboard is handy when you want to keep an eye on your web server; just continually refresh the page. During a spike, you are able to see new processes get spawned, switch to W to serve the request, and then, if the spike in traffic subsides, those processes slowly change to _ and ultimately . as they are no longer needed.

Generally speaking, when you access the server status page, you do so from the command line while logged into the web server. This lets you restrict what hosts can view the page while still providing all the information you need. Now, by default, if you were to run curl against the regular server status page, you would get HTML output. However, if you pass the auto option to the server-status page, you will get text output that's more useful for both command-line viewing and parsing by scripts:

```
$ curl http://localhost/server-status?auto
  % Total    % Received % Xferd  Average Speed   Time    Time     Time  Current
                                 Dload  Upload   Total   Spent    Left  Speed
117   586  117   586    0     0   2579      0 --:--:-- --:--:-- --:--:--  2579117   586  11
7   586    0     0   1905      0 --:--:-- --:--:-- --:--:--      0
Total Accesses: 2343235
Total kBytes: 265925501
CPULoad: .0773742
Uptime: 6801454
ReqPerSec: .34452
BytesPerSec: 40036.7
BytesPerReq: 116210
BusyWorkers: 53
IdleWorkers: 28
Scoreboard: WW_W__W_W__W_K_W_W_K___WWWWW_WWKWWWW_WWWWWWWWWWWWWWWWWWKKKKKK_KW_.WC.CW_____K__
____.....................................................................................
.........................................................................................
.........................................................................................
.........................................
```

When you want to monitor the status page of a server in the command line, although you could just run the curl command over and over, you could use a handy command called watch, which will run whatever command you specify every *x* number of seconds (by default 2). So if you wanted to keep an eye on the status page and have it refresh every 5 seconds on the command line, you would type

```
$ watch -n 5 'curl http://localhost/server-status?auto'
```

To exit out of watch, just hit Ctrl-C.

Solve Common Web Server Problems

Although it's difficult to document how to solve any and all web server problems, you are likely to run into a few general classes of problems that have identifiable symptoms. This section will highlight some of the common types of problems you may find, their symptoms, and how to remedy them.

Configuration Problems

One common and relatively simple problem to identify in a web server is a configuration problem. Since web servers need to be reloaded to take on changes in their configuration, it can be tempting to make many changes without reloading the web server; however, if you do so, you are likely to find out during a server maintenance (or when you need to restart the server to load new SSL certificates) that there's some syntax error in your configuration files and your server will refuse to start.

Both Apache and Nginx validate their configuration files when you start, restart, or reload the service, so that's one way to find configuration errors— unfortunately, it also means that in the case of a problem, the server is down while you fix the errors. Fortunately, both web servers provide means to test configuration syntax and highlight any syntax errors while the server is still running.

In the case of Apache, the command is apache2ctl configtest. Be sure to run this command as a user who can read all of the configuration files (probably the root user). A successful run looks like this:

```
$ sudo apache2ctl configtest
Syntax OK
```

When there is a syntax error, this command will identify the file and line number of the error so it's easy to find:

```
$ sudo apache2ctl configtest
apache2: Syntax error on line 233 of /etc/apache2/apache2.conf: Could not open configuration
  ➥file /etc/apache2/conf/: No such file or directory
```

In this case, the configuration file had a typo—the directory you wanted to include was /etc/apache2/conf.d.

Nginx also provides a syntax check by running nginx -t:

```
$ sudo nginx -t
the configuration file /etc/nginx/nginx.conf syntax is ok
configuration file /etc/nginx/nginx.conf test is successful
```

As with Apache, when Nginx detects an error, it tells you the file and line number:

```
$ sudo nginx -t
[emerg]: unknown directive "included" in /etc/nginx/nginx.conf:13
configuration file /etc/nginx/nginx.conf test failed
```

Permissions Problems

A common headache, especially for new web server administrators, is permission problems on the web server. Although both Apache and Nginx's initial processes run as root, all subprocesses that actually do the work of serving content run as a user with more restricted permissions—usually a user like www-data or apache. If you are, for instance, uploading web pages as a different user, you may initially run into permissions problems until you make sure that each file you want to serve is readable by the www-data or apache user.

So what does a permissions problem look like from the outside? This example takes a basic Nginx setup and changes the permissions on the main index.html file so that it is no longer readable by the world. Then it uses curl to attempt to load the page:

```
$ curl http://localhost
<html>
<head><title>403 Forbidden</title></head>
<body bgcolor="white">
<center><h1>403 Forbidden</h1></center>
<hr><center>nginx/0.7.65</center>
</body>
</html>
```

The output from the web page tells us the HTTP error even without having to tell curl to display it: a 403 Forbidden error. Unfortunately, although we can see the page is forbidden, from this output, we're not yet sure why. At this point, though, we would turn to the Nginx error logs and see

```
2012/07/07 16:13:37 [error] 547#0: *2 open() "/var/www/nginx-default/index.html" failed
  ↪(13: Permission denied), client: 127.0.0.1, server: localhost, request: "GET /
  ↪HTTP/1.1", host: "localhost"
```

This error log lets us know that Nginx attempted to open /var/www/nginx-default/index.html, but permission was denied. At this point, we could check out the permissions of that file and confirm that it wasn't readable by the www-data user Nginx runs as:

```
$ ps -ef | grep nginx
root       545    1  0 15:19 ?        00:00:00 nginx: master process /usr/sbin/nginx
www-data   547  545  0 15:19 ?        00:00:00 nginx: worker process

$ ls -l /var/www/nginx-default/index.html
-rw-r----- 1 root root 151 2006-08-30 03:39 /var/www/nginx-default/index.html
```

In this case, you could fix this permission problem with the chmod o+r command, which would add world read permissions to the file. Alternatively, you could also change the group ownership of the file so it was owned by the www-data group (or by a group that www-data was a member of).

Although some administrators may sidestep permissions problems by basically making all files readable and writeable by everyone, the security risks of doing so aren't worth the easy fix. Instead, consider creating a group on the system whose membership includes both www-data or apache users (depending on what user your web server runs as) and the users you upload files as. If you do try the "chmod 777" method of making the file readable by everyone, use it only as a temporary sanity check to confirm that the problem truly is a permissions issue. Be sure after you have solved the problem to change permissions back to something more secure.

Sluggish or Unavailable Web Server

Although configuration and permission problems are pretty well defined, probably one of the more common web server problems you will troubleshoot is nice and vague—the server seems slow to the point it may even be temporarily unavailable. Although a large number of root causes make this kind of problem, this section will guide you through some common causes for sluggish web servers along with their symptoms.

High Load   One of the first things I check when a server is sluggish or temporarily unavailable is its load. If you haven't already read through Chapter 2, read it to learn how to determine whether the server is suffering from high load, and if so, whether that high load is the result of your web server processes; if it is, you'll learn how to determine whether the load is CPU, RAM, or I/O bound.

Once you have identified whether the load is high and that your web server processes are the issue, if the load is CPU-bound, then you will likely need to troubleshoot any CGIs, PHP code, and so on, that your web server executes to generate dynamic content. Go through your web server logs and attempt to identify which pages are being accessed during this high load period; then attempt to load them yourself (possibly on a test server if your main server is overloaded) to gauge how much CPU various dynamic pages consume.

If the load seems RAM-bound and you notice you are using more and more swap storage and may even completely run out of RAM, then you may be facing the dreaded web server swap death spiral. This shows up commonly in Apache prefork servers but could potentially show up in Apache worker or even Nginx servers in the right conditions. Essentially, when you configure your web server, you can configure the maximum number of web server instances the server will spawn in response to traffic. In Apache prefork, this is known as the MaxClient setting. When a server gets so much traffic that it spawns more web server processes than can fit in RAM, processes end up using the much slower swap space instead. This causes those processes to respond much more slowly than processes residing in RAM, which causes the requests to take longer, which in turn causes more processes to be needed to handle the current load until, ultimately, both RAM and swap are consumed.

To solve this issue, you will need to calculate how many web server processes can fit into RAM. First calculate how much RAM an individual web server process will take, then take your total RAM and subtract your operating system overhead. Then figure out how many Apache processes you currently can fit into the remaining free RAM without going into swap. You should then configure your web server so it never launches more processes than it can fit into RAM.

Of course, with modern dynamically generated web pages, setting this value can be a bit tricky. After all, some PHP scripts, for instance, use little RAM whereas others may use quite a bit. In circumstances like this, the best tactic is to look at all of the web server processes on a busy web server and attempt to gauge the maximum, minimum, and average amount of RAM a process consumes. Then you can decide whether to set the number of web servers according to the worst case (maximum amount of RAM) or the average case.

If your load is I/O bound, and the web server has a database back-end on the same machine, you might simply be saturating your disk I/O with database requests. Of course, if you followed the load troubleshooting guide from Chapter 2, you should have been able to identify database processes as the culprit instead of web server processes. In either case, you may want to consider either putting your database on a separate server, upgrading your storage speed, or going to Chapter 9 for more information on how to troubleshoot database issues. Even if the database server is on a separate machine, each web server process that is waiting on a response from the database over the network may still generate a high load average.

Otherwise, if the server is I/O bound but the problem seems to be coming from the web server itself and not the database, it could be that the software that powers your website running on the machine simply is saturating disk I/O with requests. Alternatively, if you have enabled reverse DNS resolution in your logs so that IP addresses are converted into hostnames, your web server processes could simply have to wait on each DNS query to resolve before it finishes its request.

Server Status Pages One of the other main places to look when diagnosing sluggish servers, other than troubleshooting high load on the system, is in the server status page. Earlier in the chapter we talked about how to enable and view the server status page in your web server. In cases of slow or unavailable web servers, this status page gives a nice overall view of the health of your web server. You not only see system load averages, you can also see how many processes are currently busy and what they are doing.

If, for instance, you see something like this,

```
$ curl http://localhost/server-status?auto
. . .
Scoreboard: WWWWWWWWWWWWWKWWWWWKWWWWWWWWWWWKWWWWWWWWWWWWWWWWWWWWWWWWKKKKKKWKWWWWCWCWWWWWWKWW
____WWWWWWWWWWWWWWWWWWWWWWWWWWWWWWWWWWWWWWWWWWWWWWWWWWWWWWWWWWWWWWWWWWWWWWWWWWWWWWWWWW
WWWWWWWWWWWWWWWWWWWWWWWWWWWWWWWWWWWWWWWWWWWWWWWWWWWWWWWWWWWWWWWWWWWWWWWWWWWWWWWWWWWWWW
WWWWWWWWWWWWWWWWWWWWWWWWWWWWWWWWWWWWWWWWWWWWWWWWWWWWWWWWWWWWWWWWWWWWWWWWWWWWWWWWWWWWWW
WWWWWWWWWWWWWWWWWWWWWWWWWWWWWWWWWWWWWWWWWWWWWWW
```

you'll know that this server is completely overloaded with requests. As you refresh this page, you may see a process open up every now and then, but clearly, just about every process is busy fulfilling a request. In this circumstance, you may just need to allow your web server to spawn more processes (if you can fit them in RAM), or, alternatively, it may be time to add another web server to help share the load.

Then again, if you see a scoreboard like the one shown earlier, but notice that your web server seems quite responsive, it could be that each web request is having to wait on something on the back end. Behavior like this can happen when an application server is overloaded with waiting requests (sometimes because, ultimately, the database server it depends on is overloaded), so although all the web server processes are busy, adding more wouldn't necessarily help the issue—they would also still be waiting on the back end to respond.

On the other hand, you might see something like this:

```
Scoreboard: WW_W__W_W__W_K_W_W_K___WWWWW_WWKWWWW_WWWWWWWWWWWWWWWWWKKKKKK_KW_.WC.CW_____K__
____.......................................................................................
...........................................................................................
...........................................................................................
...........................................
```

This is a server that has many processes to spare, both ones that are loaded into RAM and ones that are waiting to be loaded. If your server is sluggish but your scoreboard looks like this, then you are going to need to dig into your web server logs and try to identify which pages are currently being loaded. Ultimately you will want to identify which pages on your site are taking so long to respond, and then you'll need to dig into that software to try to find the root cause. Of course, it could also simply be that your web server is underpowered for the software it's running, and if so, it's time to consider a hardware upgrade.

## CHAPTER 9

Why Is the Database Slow? Tracking Down Database Problems

IT'S A RARE DevOps team that never encounters databases. An application that reaches a certain level of complexity will certainly store its data in some sort of database. Due to the prevalence of database wrapper libraries, the ease of installation of some of the more popular databases, and the general familiarity developers have with SQL, often even relatively simple applications store data in a database and retrieve it via SQL commands. It's the rare website that is purely static data. Most provide some sort of dynamic content to the user, and many, including the popular blogging platforms, store all of the relevant content in a database. Whether your company has dedicated database administrators or not, everyone on the DevOps team can benefit from some basic database troubleshooting skills. After all, your DBA (database administrator) may not be responsible for the database backing your wiki, your build environment, or the test environment you run on your laptop.

It's true that in the modern DevOps world, traditional SQL-based databases are not nearly as popular as they once were. It seems like there's a new NoSQL-style database coming out every week. Discussing how to troubleshoot all of the popular SQL-based databases and the NoSQL databases would fill a complete book (or two); so instead, this chapter is going to simply cover the two most popular Open Source SQL-based databases you are most likely to run into: MySQL and PostgresSQL. Each major section of this chapter will introduce a particular troubleshooting technique and then describe how it applies to MySQL and then PostgresSQL. By the end of the chapter, you should be able to identify whether a database is running and listening on the right ports, pull performance metrics, and identify slow queries in a database.

Search Database Logs

One of the places you should look when troubleshooting a database issue is the error log for that database, particularly if there is a problem with the database starting. The error log also often provides information about successful startup and syntax errors in queries sent to the database; these are particularly useful when you are debugging applications.

MySQL

For MySQL, depending on your distribution, you might find this error log directly in /var/log, under /var/log/mysql, or maybe even under /var/lib/mysql. Here's some example output from a MySQL startup in /var/log/mysql/error.log:

```
120714 15:35:26 [Note] Plugin 'FEDERATED' is disabled.
120714 15:35:26  InnoDB: Initializing buffer pool, size = 8.0M
120714 15:35:26  InnoDB: Completed initialization of buffer pool
120714 15:35:26  InnoDB: Started; log sequence number 0 67138180
120714 15:35:27 [Note] Event Scheduler: Loaded 0 events
120714 15:35:27 [Note] /usr/sbin/mysqld: ready for connections.
Version: '5.1.63-0ubuntu0.10.04.1-log'  socket: '/var/run/mysqld/mysqld.sock'  port: 3306
  ➥(Ubuntu)
```

PostgresSQL

For PostgresSQL, your distribution might put the logs in /var/log or in /var/log/postgresql. Here is some sample output from my /var/log/postgresql/postgresql-8.4-main.log, including a syntax error:

```
2012-07-10 20:08:07 PDT LOG:     database system is ready to accept connections
2012-07-10 20:08:07 PDT LOG:     autovacuum launcher started
2012-07-10 20:08:07 PDT LOG:     incomplete startup packet
2012-07-11 14:15:48 PDT LOG:     incomplete startup packet
2012-07-11 14:16:01 PDT LOG:     incomplete startup packet
2012-07-12 05:06:53 PDT ERROR:  operator does not exist: name = pg_stat_all_tables at
  ➥character 47
2012-07-12 05:06:53 PDT HINT:   No operator matches the given name and argument type(s).
  ➥You might need to add explicit type casts.
```

High Server Load

Before we get into database-specific steps, if you are trying to troubleshoot a slow database server that has high load, particularly if that server does more than just run database software, check out the tips in Chapter 2 for how to diagnose the cause of high load. The steps in that chapter should not only help you determine whether the database is the real cause of the load, but also help you figure out whether the load is CPU-, RAM-, or IO-bound.

If a database is generating high CPU-bound load, then you might be facing a bad SQL query that is using much more processing power than it should; if this is the case, you'll want to start tracking down slow queries, which are covered later in this chapter. If your load is RAM-bound, then you will either want to tune your database to take on fewer simultaneous queries or attempt to locate particularly expensive SQL queries that tie up RAM (or stop storing your database on your RAM disk). If the load is IO-bound, then use tools like iotop to try to identify which specific process, and sysstat to locate which storage, is getting hit the most. Of course, in all of these cases, you may also just need to upgrade your hardware or add another server to your cluster.

Is the Database Running?

One of the very first things you will want to check if there seems to be a database problem is whether the database is running and listening on the right port. Although you can test whether the port is available remotely, the best way to truly test whether the database process is running and listening on the right port is from the server itself. That said, refer to Chapter 5 for more information on how to perform network troubleshooting if you suspect a network issue may prevent you from connecting to your database. Both MySQL and PostgresSQL have quite different sets of processes, and they both listen on different ports.

MySQL

There are a few different ways to test whether MySQL is running. First, you can use its init script as it supports the status command. The benefit here is that you don't really need to know what the name of the process is, just the name of the init script located in /etc/rc.d/init.d/ or /etc/init.d/. In the case of a Debian-based system, the service is called mysql, so you can pull the status with

```
$ sudo service mysql status
mysql start/running, process 735
```

You can also confirm that MySQL is running using a combination of ps and grep:

```
$ ps -ef | grep mysql
mysql     735    1 0 Jun12 ?        02:02:56 /usr/sbin/mysqld
```

Notice that the process ID that the status command returned (735) matches what you get from ps. Of course, if MySQL is running but listening to the wrong port (or only listening on localhost and you need it to listen on all interfaces), you still may not be able to connect to it even though it is running. So next you will want to test that MySQL is listening on the correct port. By default, MySQL should listen on port 3306; of course, if you have configured it to listen on a different port, you will need to change the following command to match your environment. The netstat command, when passed the -lnp options, will display all ports that are in a listening state along with the process that has that port open:

```
$ sudo netstat -lnp | grep :3306
tcp       0    0 127.0.0.1:3306        0.0.0.0:*              LISTEN      735/mysqld
```

Again, notice that the MySQL process in the output has the same process ID (735) as in the earlier commands. If you don't get any output from this command, then there is no process listening on port 3306. You may want to just view the output of netstat with no grep (or grep for mysql instead) and see if any processes come up. In this example, it's also worth noting that the MySQL process is listening only on localhost (127.0.0.1:3306), which is fine since the web service that accesses it is located on the same server. However, if you needed to access MySQL from another machine and you got this output, you would want to reconfigure MySQL so it listens either on the IP of your network interface or on all interfaces (0.0.0.0).

PostgresSQL

As with MySQL, you can query the init script or use ps to test whether PostgresSQL is running, but depending on your system, the PostgresSQL init script may have a different name. For instance, on Debian-based systems like Ubuntu, the init script is named after the version of PostgresSQL, so you would run

```
$ sudo service postgresql-8.4 status
Running clusters: 8.4/main
```

Substitute postgresql-8.4 for postgresql-9.1 or whatever version you have installed on your system, or just check the /etc/init.d or /etc/rc.d/init.d directories if you aren't sure about the name of the init script.

Alternatively, you can use the ps command:

```
$ ps -ef | grep postgres
postgres  1629     1  0 Jul10 ?        00:00:06 /usr/lib/postgresql/8.4/bin/postgres -D /
   ↪var/lib/postgresql/8.4/main -c config_file=/etc/postgresql/8.4/main/postgresql.conf
postgres  1631  1629  0 Jul10 ?        00:00:38 postgres: writer process
postgres  1632  1629  0 Jul10 ?        00:00:30 postgres: wal writer process
postgres  1633  1629  0 Jul10 ?        00:00:08 postgres: autovacuum launcher process
postgres  1634  1629  0 Jul10 ?        00:00:04 postgres: stats collector process
```

Unlike with MySQL, with PostgresSQL, even a basic install has multiple processes running and being responsible for different tasks. Also, since PostgresSQL listens on a different port (5432) by default than MySQL, when you run netstat, you will need to grep for that port:

```
$ sudo netstat -lnp | grep :5432
tcp       0      0 127.0.0.1:5432        0.0.0.0:*              LISTEN      1629/postgres
tcp6      0      0 ::1:5432              :::*                   LISTEN      1629/postgres
```

Note here that the process that is listening on the port has the same process ID (1629) as the first process in the ps output. If you don't get any output, try grepping for postgres instead of the port to see if postgres is listening on any other port (or just look at the netstat output without the grep command). Also note that in this case PostgresSQL is listening only on the localhost IP (127.0.0.1:5432), so only processes on the same server can access the database—a safe default if that's all you need. If you do need other servers to be able to access the database and PostgresSQL is only listening on 127.0.0.1, you will need to reconfigure PostgresSQL to either listen on the IP for the network interface you want to use or have it listen for all interfaces (0.0.0.0).

Get Database Metrics

When you are trying to track down a problem with your database, server metrics can be useful, but even more useful are metrics from the database itself. Both MySQL and PostgresSQL give you access to their metrics, but as you'll see, they do it in completely different ways.

MySQL

To pull metrics from MySQL, you'll use the mysqladmin tool, which should be installed as part of the MySQL client software on your system (this also means you can install that software on a different system, potentially connect to the database over the network, and pull this data). The most basic (and possibly most immediately useful) data we will pull with mysqladmin is with the status command:

```
mysqladmin -u root -p status
Enter password:
Uptime: 2680987  Threads: 1  Questions: 17494181  Slow queries: 0  Opens: 2096  Flush
 ➥tables: 1  Open tables: 64  Queries per second avg: 6.525
```

Here is what each of these values represents, pulled from the mysqladmin man page:

* **Uptime**

  The number of seconds the MySQL server has been running

* **Threads**

  The number of active threads (clients)

* **Questions**

  The number of questions (queries) from clients since the server was started

※ **Slow queries**

The number of queries that have taken more than `long_query_time` seconds

※ **Opens**

The number of tables the server has opened

※ **Flush tables**

The number of flush-*, refresh, and reload commands the server has executed

※ **Open tables**

The number of tables that currently are open

※ **Queries per second avg**

The average number of queries per second the database receives

For a lot of your database troubleshooting, these values may be enough for you to build a baseline and tell when some number is out of the norm, in particular the threads, slow queries, and queries-per-second metrics. Of course, if you want more in-depth information, you can get that too—via the extended-status command:

```
$ mysqladmin -u root -p extended-status
Enter password:
+-----------------------------------+-------------+
| Variable_name                     | Value       |
+-----------------------------------+-------------+
| Aborted_clients                   | 0           |
| Aborted_connects                  | 5           |
| Binlog_cache_disk_use             | 0           |
| Binlog_cache_use                  | 0           |
| Bytes_received                    | 3264109643  |
| Bytes_sent                        | 49337359253 |

. . .
| Threads_cached                    | 7           |
| Threads_connected                 | 1           |
| Threads_created                   | 6575        |
| Threads_running                   | 1           |
| Uptime                            | 2683061     |
| Uptime_since_flush_status         | 2683061     |
+-----------------------------------+-------------+
```

The extended-status command will give you all of the information from the status command plus a huge number of other metrics that you can use to help build a baseline for your database so that you can see when things fall outside of the norm.

PostgresSQL

PostgresSQL collects and lists performance statistics in a much different way than MySQL. First you need to edit your postgresql.conf file (for example, on an Ubuntu system, this is located at /etc/postgresql/8.4/main/) and make sure that the track_activities and track_counts options are set to on. They likely default to on, but if you need to change these variables, you will need to restart PostgresSQL afterward for the changes to take effect.

Once statistics collection is enabled, the data will be stored in special tables in the database. Unlike with MySQL, you will use SQL commands to pull this data out of those tables. The complete list of statistics tables is documented in the official PostgresSQL documentation, but the following sections will list a few of the particularly useful tables. First though, be sure to become the postgres user (or another user who has superuser permissions on the database) so you can send your queries:

```
# su - postgres
$ psql
psql (8.4.12)
Type "help" for help.
```

pg_stat_activity   The pg_stat_activity table displays information about each currently running server process including which database it is accessing, which system process it uses, which user is accessing it, the current query, and data about how long the query has been running. This table is particularly valuable when you know a particular database process is using a lot of CPU time and you want to know what query it is in the middle of. To see all of the data in the table, use a standard select statement:

```
postgres=# select * from pg_stat_activity;
 datid | datname  | procpid | usesysid | usename  |           current_query
       | waiting  |            xact_start           |          query_start           |
           backend_start           | client_addr | client_port
-------+----------+---------+----------+----------+---------------------------
----+----------+----------------------------+---------------------------+-
--------------------------------+-------------+-------------
 11564 | postgres |    4689 |       10 | postgres | select * from pg_stat_activi
ty; | f       | 2012-07-12 04:26:19.602872-07 | 2012-07-12 04:26:19.602872-07 |
2012-07-12 04:26:01.363883-07 |             |          -1
(1 row)
```

In this example, you can see the default PostgresSQL database isn't doing all that much—the only process is the one you initiated to pull statistics. However, if you were trying to track down a particular process, all you would have to do is modify your SQL statement:

```
postgres=# select * from pg_stat_activity where procpid=4689;
 datid | datname  | procpid | usesysid | usename  |          current_query
       |            | waiting  |          xact_start           |          query_start           |
           backend_start           | client_addr | client_port
-------+----------+---------+----------+----------+---------------------------
----+----------+----------------------------+---------------------------+-
--------------------------------+-------------+-------------
 11564 | postgres |    4689 |       10 | postgres | select * from pg_stat_activi
ty where procpid=4689; | f       | 2012-07-12 04:26:19.602872-07 | 2012-07-12 04:26:19.602872-07 |
2012-07-12 04:26:01.363883-07 |             |          -1
(1 row)
```

pg_stat_database   The pg_stat_database table stores database statistics, such as the number of server processes connected to that database, the number of transactions committed and rolled back, and block and row statistics. Like with pg_stat_activity, a basic select statement can pull all of the current data:

```
postgres=# select * from pg_stat_database;
 datid |  datname  | numbackends | xact_commit | xact_rollback | blks_read | blk
s_hit | tup_returned | tup_fetched | tup_inserted | tup_updated | tup_deleted
```

```
-------+-----------+-------------+----------------+---------------+-----------+----
------+--------------+-------------+--------------+---------------+-------------+--------------
     1 | template1 |           0 |              0 |             0 |         0 |
     0 |            0 |           0 |            0 |             0 |           0
 11563 | template0 |           0 |              0 |             0 |         0 |
     0 |            0 |           0 |            0 |             0 |           0
 11564 | postgres  |           1 |           3876 |             0 |       116 |
 61544 |    1075635 |        6775 |            0 |             0 |           0
(3 rows)
```

This example is from a default PostgresSQL install so the default databases are listed, but you would also see any databases you have created as well.

pg_stat_all_tables   The pg_stat_all_tables table stores statistics on a per-table basis including sequential scan statistics, index scan statistics, and data about the number of other operations performed on that table. Since this stores data on all the existing tables, the default select will return a lot of data:

```
postgres=# select * from pg_stat_all_tables;
 relid  |    schemaname     |          relname         | seq_scan | seq_tup_read
 | idx_scan | idx_tup_fetch | n_tup_ins | n_tup_upd | n_tup_del | n_tup_hot_upd |
 n_live_tup | n_dead_tup | last_vacuum | last_autovacuum | last_analyze | last_a
utoanalyze
-------+-------------------+--------------------------+----------+---------------
+----------+---------------+-----------+-----------+-----------+---------------+
-----------+------------+-------------+-----------------+--------------+--------
-----------
  2753 | pg_catalog        | pg_opfamily              |        0 |            0
 |        0 |             0 |         0 |         0 |         0 |             0 |
         0 |          0 |             |                 |              |
  2617 | pg_catalog        | pg_operator              |        0 |            0
 |        7 |             7 |         0 |         0 |         0 |             0 |
         0 |          0 |             |                 |              |
. . .
  2328 | pg_catalog        | pg_foreign_data_wrapper  |        0 |            0
 |        0 |             0 |         0 |         0 |         0 |             0 |
         0 |          0 |             |                 |              |
(65 rows)
```

This is definitely an example where you might want to prune the output with specific SQL queries to get the data you want. Of course, it may just be that you want to exclude all of the system tables and only list user tables; view the pg_stat_user_tables table to just see user tables or the pg_stat_sys_tables to just see system tables.

Identify Slow Queries

When debugging problems with a database, one of the most common questions you'll have to answer is "Why is the database slow?" To answer that question, you'll want to be able to identify any slow queries—database queries that take longer than a certain threshold. When you can identify slow queries, you can then work on optimizing them to run faster on your database. Both MySQL and PostgresSQL have mechanisms in place to log slow queries so that you can view them later.

MySQL

To enable slow query logging in MySQL, you will need to set two variables: log_slow_queries and long_query_time. The log_slow_queries variable should be set to the file you want to log all of your slow queries to (make sure the user MySQL runs as can write to this location), and long_query_time should be set to the threshold in seconds for how long a query needs to take to be considered a slow query. In the default my.cnf file that came with the MySQL installation, these settings were already present in the file; they were just commented out:

```
# Here you can see queries with especially long duration
log_slow_queries = /var/log/mysql/mysql-slow.log
long_query_time = 2
```

Once you set both of these values, you will need to restart the MySQL process. When you do, notice that it creates the slow query log for you when it restarts; the contents look something like this:

```
/usr/sbin/mysqld, Version: 5.1.63-0ubuntu0.10.04.1-log ((Ubuntu)). started with:
Tcp port: 3306  Unix socket: /var/run/mysqld/mysqld.sock
Time                Id Command    Argument
```

As queries come up that take longer than your threshold, you will be able to see them in this log along with information about the query, such as the user who executed it, the query and lock times, how many rows were sent, and how many were examined. You can then use this information to go back to your application, identify where that query originates, and find ways to optimize it.

Another way to identify problem MySQL queries is via the mysqladmin processlist command, which lists information about all the currently active MySQL processes. Here's some sample output from a relatively inactive WordPress install that had one client (a local mysql client connection) connected along with this mysqladmin command:

```
$ mysqladmin -u root -p processlist
Enter password:
+------+------+-----------+-----------+---------+------+-------+------------------+
| Id   | User | Host      | db        | Command | Time | State | Info             |
+------+------+-----------+-----------+---------+------+-------+------------------+
| 2663 | root | localhost | wordpress | Sleep   | 80   |       |                  |
| 2686 | root | localhost |           | Query   | 0    |       | show processlist |
+------+------+-----------+-----------+---------+------+-------+------------------+
```

You can also add the -i option along with the number of seconds; when you do, this command will execute over and over with that number of seconds gap in between. Then you can monitor commands as they come in and identify any queries that are taking much longer than they should. If you do identify a query that is slowing down the system and you want to kill it, make a note of the process ID in the output of the processlist command, and use the kill command along with that process ID to kill the process. For instance, if you wanted to kill the above connection to the WordPress DB that had been connected for 80 seconds, you would type

```
$ mysqladmin -u root -p kill 2663
```

PostgresSQL

PostgresSQL gives you the option to log all queries, not just those that are above a certain threshold with the log_min_duration_statement setting. If this value is set to -1, then no queries are logged. If it is set to 0, then all queries are logged. If it is set to anything greater than zero, then it will log all queries that take longer than that number in milliseconds. So, for instance, to log all queries that take longer than 100 milliseconds, you would set the value like this:

```
log_min_duration_statement = 100
```

Once set, restart the PostgresSQL service so the settings take effect. You should then start to see any queries that take longer than your threshold to show up in the logs. Remember that unlike MySQL, PostgresSQL expects this value to be in milliseconds, not seconds. Be careful not to set the threshold too low, though, unless you want to slow down your database by logging everything. For instance, setting the value to 1 will even pick up statistics-gathering queries in the log:

```
2012-07-12 11:02:00 PDT LOG:  duration: 28.964 ms  statement: select * from
  ↪pg_stat_activity;
2012-07-12 11:02:12 PDT LOG:  duration: 39.845 ms  statement: select * from
  ↪pg_stat_all_tables;
```

## CHAPTER 10

It's the Hardware's Fault! Diagnosing Common Hardware Problems

THE WORLD OF DevOps is largely a world of software, but ultimately that software needs to run on a physical machine and that physical machine can have its own host of problems. Although if you are a developer or work in QA, you may think that hardware is the sysadmin's domain; since everyone in DevOps organizations works much more closely together, having hardware troubleshooting skills is invaluable. After all, no matter who is responsible for the hardware, if you could find out ahead of time that the hard drive on an important server is about to fail, wouldn't you want to know? If you knew that your network application was failing not because of bugs in your code, but because the network card was faulty, you might save yourself hours or days of debugging. If your application crashes randomly, your code may be fine and it could be a bad stick of RAM.

This chapter will cover some of the more common hardware failures you might run into, along with steps to troubleshoot and confirm them. It starts with some of the more common pieces of hardware that fail—hard drives and RAM—and then continues with how to troubleshoot some other common hardware problems.

The Hard Drive Is Dying

Many different components make up a server, but consistently the hard drives seem to be the weakest link. If any piece of hardware is going to fail before its time, it will likely be a hard drive. That's why so many servers have some sort of redundancy in the form of RAID. Although hard drive manufacturers all have their own hard drive testing tools, modern hard drives should also support SMART, which monitors the overall health of the hard drive and can alert you when the drive will fail soon. Unlike with a lot of vendor tools, you can check the health of your hard drive via SMART without rebooting.

SMART tools should be available for any major Linux distribution, so just use your package manager and search for the keyword "smart." Under Debian-based distributions, for instance, the package is called smartmontools. Once the package is installed, you should have a smartctl program you can run as root to scan your drives. Pass the -H option to smartctl to check the health of a drive:

```
$ sudo smartctl -H /dev/sda
smartctl version 5.37 [i686-pc-linux-gnu] Copyright (C) 2002-6 Bruce Allen
Home page is http://smartmontools.sourceforge.net/
SMART Health Status: OK
```

In this example, the hard drive is healthy, but smartctl may also return either failures or warnings about a drive:

```
$ sudo smartctl -H /dev/sda
smartctl version 5.38 [x86_64-unknown-linux-gnu] Copyright (C) 2002-8 Bruce Allen
Home page is http://smartmontools.sourceforge.net/

=== START OF READ SMART DATA SECTION ===
SMART overall-health self-assessment test result: PASSED
Please note the following marginal Attributes:
ID# ATTRIBUTE_NAME          FLAG    VALUE WORST THRESH TYPE     UPDATED  WHEN_FAILED  RAW_VALUE
190 Airflow_Temperature_Cel 0x0022  056   037   045    Old_age  Always   In_the_past  44
    ↪(Lifetime Min/Max 20/50)
```

In this case, the drive passed but returned a warning about airflow temperature for the drive (it's in an enclosure that probably could use better airflow). Both examples pointed smartctl at /dev/sda, the first SCSI drive in the system, so you may need to change that to /dev/sdb or another device to check all of your drives. If you are unsure of the drives in your system, look at the output of sudo fdisk -l. It will list all of the disks and partitions it can detect, but keep in mind that it will also show virtual drives like any software RAID partitions (/dev/mdX devices) you have set up.

You can also pull much more information about a hard drive using smartctl with the -a option. That option will pull out all of the SMART information about the drive in one fell swoop:

```
$ sudo smartctl -a /dev/sda
smartctl version 5.38 [x86_64-unknown-linux-gnu] Copyright (C) 2002-8 Bruce Allen
Home page is http://smartmontools.sourceforge.net/
```

```
=== START OF INFORMATION SECTION ===
Model Family:     Seagate Barracuda 7200.10 family
Device Model:     ST3400620AS
Serial Number:    3QH01QZ3
Firmware Version: 3.AAD
User Capacity:    400,088,457,216 bytes
Device is:        In smartctl database [for details use: -P show]
ATA Version is:   7
ATA Standard is:  Exact ATA specification draft version not indicated
Local Time is:    Sun Jul 15 14:03:44 2012 PDT
SMART support is: Available - device has SMART capability.
SMART support is: Enabled

=== START OF READ SMART DATA SECTION ===
SMART overall-health self-assessment test result: PASSED
See vendor-specific Attribute list for marginal Attributes.

General SMART Values:
Offline data collection status:  (0x82) Offline data collection activity
                                        was completed without error.
                                        Auto Offline Data Collection: Enabled.
Self-test execution status:      (   0) The previous self-test routine completed
                                        without error or no self-test has ever
                                        been run.
Total time to complete Offline
data collection:                 ( 430) seconds.
Offline data collection
capabilities:                    (0x5b) SMART execute Offline immediate.
                                        Auto Offline data collection on/off support.
                                        Suspend Offline collection upon new
                                        command.
                                        Offline surface scan supported.
                                        Self-test supported.
                                        No Conveyance Self-test supported.
                                        Selective Self-test supported.
SMART capabilities:            (0x0003) Saves SMART data before entering
                                        power-saving mode.
                                        Supports SMART auto save timer.
Error logging capability:        (0x01) Error logging supported.
                                        General Purpose Logging supported.
Short self-test routine
recommended polling time:        (   1) minutes.
Extended self-test routine
recommended polling time:        ( 132) minutes.
```

```
SMART Attributes Data Structure revision number: 10
Vendor Specific SMART Attributes with Thresholds:
ID# ATTRIBUTE_NAME          FLAG    VALUE WORST THRESH TYPE      UPDATED  WHEN_FAILED  RAW_VALUE
  1 Raw_Read_Error_Rate     0x000f  120   093   006    Pre-fail  Always   -            242629896
  3 Spin_Up_Time            0x0003  085   085   000    Pre-fail  Always   -            0
  4 Start_Stop_Count        0x0032  100   100   020    Old_age   Always   -            46
  5 Reallocated_Sector_Ct   0x0033  100   100   036    Pre-fail  Always   -            0
  7 Seek_Error_Rate         0x000f  075   060   030    Pre-fail  Always   -            33428869
  9 Power_On_Hours          0x0032  062   062   000    Old_age   Always   -            33760
 10 Spin_Retry_Count        0x0013  100   100   097    Pre-fail  Always   -            0
 12 Power_Cycle_Count       0x0032  100   100   020    Old_age   Always   -            67
187 Reported_Uncorrect      0x0032  100   100   000    Old_age   Always   -            0
189 High_Fly_Writes         0x003a  100   100   000    Old_age   Always   -            0
190 Airflow_Temperature_Cel 0x0022  060   037   045    Old_age   Always   In_the_past  40
  ↪(Lifetime Min/Max 20/50)
194 Temperature_Celsius     0x0022  040   063   000    Old_age   Always   -            40
  ↪(0 16 0 0)
195 Hardware_ECC_Recovered  0x001a  065   057   000    Old_age   Always   -            35507735
197 Current_Pending_Sector  0x0012  100   100   000    Old_age   Always   -            0
198 Offline_Uncorrectable   0x0010  100   100   000    Old_age   Offline  -            0
199 UDMA_CRC_Error_Count    0x003e  200   200   000    Old_age   Always   -            68
200 Multi_Zone_Error_Rate   0x0000  100   253   000    Old_age   Offline  -            0
202 TA_Increase_Count       0x0032  100   253   000    Old_age   Always   -            0

SMART Error Log Version: 1
No Errors Logged

SMART Self-test log structure revision number 1

SMART Selective self-test log data structure revision number 1
 SPAN  MIN_LBA  MAX_LBA  CURRENT_TEST_STATUS
    1        0        0  Not_testing
    2        0        0  Not_testing
    3        0        0  Not_testing
    4        0        0  Not_testing
    5        0        0  Not_testing
Selective self-test flags (0x0):
  After scanning selected spans, do NOT read-scan remainder of disk.
If Selective self-test is pending on power-up, resume after 0 minute delay.
```

Although smartctl is useful when you just want to check the health of one drive, ideally the system could keep track of imminent failures automatically and alert you when there's a problem. The same package that provides smartctl also provides a daemon called smartd that can do this very thing. By default it may be turned off, so on a Debian-based system, you would have to edit /etc/default/smartmontools, uncomment start_smartd=yes, then run sudo service smartmontools start to start the service. If you aren't using a Debian-based distribution, check the documentation for your SMART package—it could be that the service is automatically started for you. In either case, you may want to check out the /etc/smartd.conf configuration file to tweak any default settings to suit your system.

Test RAM for Errors

Some of the most irritating types of errors to troubleshoot are those caused by bad RAM. Often errors in RAM cause random mayhem on your machine with programs crashing for no good reason, or even random kernel panics. In fact, when a once-stable server starts to misbehave, particularly with random crashes, bad RAM is one of the first things you should check.

Most major Linux distributions include an easy-to-use RAM testing tool called Memtest86+ that, in some cases, is not only installed by default, it's ready as a boot option in distributions like Ubuntu. Otherwise, install the package and you should be able to easily add it to your GRUB configuration if it isn't added automatically. Another option is to simply pick just about any Linux install disk or rescue tool. Since Memtest86+ only takes up a little bit of space, most install disks offer it as a diagnostic tool you can select at boot time. No matter how you invoke it at boot time, once you start Memtest86+, it will immediately launch and start scanning your RAM, as shown in Figure 10-1.

Memtest86+ runs through a number of exhaustive tests that can identify different types of RAM errors. At the top right, you can see which test is currently being run along with its progress; and in the Pass field, you can see how far along you are with the complete test. A thorough memory test can take hours to run, and administrators with questionable RAM might want to let the test run overnight or over multiple days if necessary to get more than one complete test through. If Memtest86+ does find

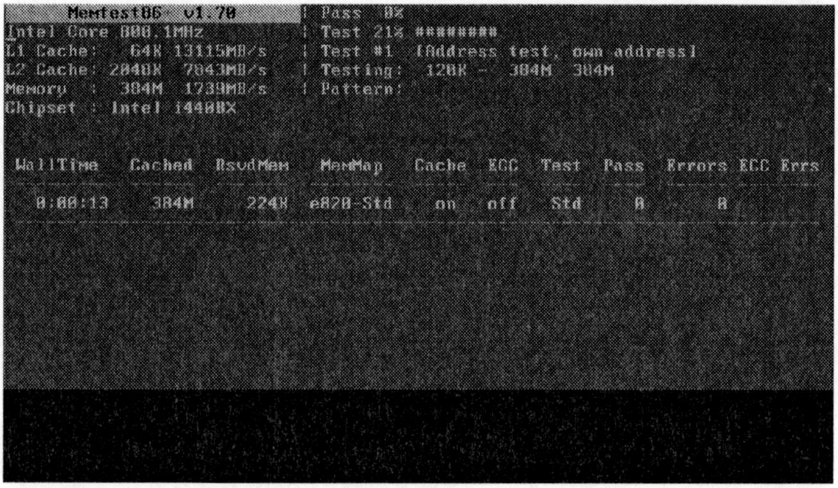

Figure 10-1 Memtest86+ testing some RAM

any errors, they will be reported in the results output at the bottom of the screen.

If you do find an error in your RAM, you may not automatically be able to identify which DIMM has the error. At this point, you will have to use the process of elimination to take out all but the minimal amount of RAM your system needs to boot (often a pair of DIMMs) and run Memtest86+ to see if that pair has an error. If the pair passes, put them in the good pile and continue on until you find a pair that has an error. Once you do, you can split the DIMM pair so you run Memtest86+ with one unknown DIMM and one known good DIMM until you can find which specific DIMM is bad. Of course, don't be lazy, and be sure to test every DIMM before you put the server back together. I've seen circumstances where two different DIMMs in the same server had problems at the same time.

Network Card Failures

When a network card starts to fail, it can be rather unnerving as you try all sorts of network troubleshooting steps to no real avail. Often when a network card or some other network component to which your host is connected starts to fail, you can see it in packet errors on your system. The ifconfig command you may have used for network troubleshooting before can also tell you about TX (transmit) or RX (receive) errors for a card. Here's an example from a healthy card:

```
$ sudo ifconfig eth0
eth0 Link encap:Ethernet HWaddr 00:17:42:1f:18:be
inet addr:10.1.1.7 Bcast:10.1.1.255 Mask:255.255.255.0
inet6 addr: fe80::217:42ff:fe1f:18be/64 Scope:Link
UP BROADCAST MULTICAST MTU:1500 Metric:1
RX packets:1 errors:0 dropped:0 overruns:0 frame:0
TX packets:11 errors:0 dropped:0 overruns:0 carrier:0
collisions:0 txqueuelen:1000
RX bytes:229 (229.0 B) TX bytes:2178 (2.1 KB)
Interrupt:10
```

The lines you are most interested in are

```
RX packets:1 errors:0 dropped:0 overruns:0 frame:0
TX packets:11 errors:0 dropped:0 overruns:0 carrier:0
collisions:0 txqueuelen:1000
```

These lines will tell you about any errors on the device. If you start to see a lot of errors here, then it's worth troubleshooting your physical network components. It's possible a network card, cable, or switch port is going bad. Start with the easiest-to-test component by swapping out the network cable with a new or known good cable, and if you continue to get errors, then move the cable to a new, hopefully known, good switch port. Finally, if neither of those solutions help, try swapping out the network card (or switching to a different port if your server has multiple Ethernet ports).

The Server Is Too Hot

Servers, especially busy servers, generate a lot of heat. Although ideally your server is colocated in a facility with good active cooling, it might also just be shoved under someone's desk, or it may sit at the top of a rack in a poorly cooled datacenter. A poorly cooled server can cause premature hard drive failure and premature failure in the rest of the server components as well. If that's not enough, modern motherboards often throttle the CPU down when it detects it is getting close to overheating, so even if your server doesn't fail completely, it may slow down to the point of being unusable. Other times, overheated components may cause processes to randomly crash.

If you suspect your datacenter may be running a bit too hot, one solution may be to purchase a rackmount thermometer that can monitor temperature for you. Rackmount thermometers work, but even if the ambient air is cool enough, a thermometer may not help you if your server is still too hot. Linux provides tools that allow you to probe CPU and motherboard temperatures, and, in some cases, the temperatures of PCI devices and even fan speeds. All of this support is provided by the lm-sensors package, which should be available for just about any distribution.

Once the lm-sensors package is installed, run the sensors-detect program as root:

```
$ sudo sensors-detect
```

This interactive script will probe the hardware on your system so it knows how to query for temperature. If you don't know how to respond to some of the questions it asks, just hit Enter to accept the default. Once the sensors-detect script is completed, you can pull data about your server by running the command sensors:

```
$ sensors
k8temp-pci-00c3
Adapter: PCI adapter
Core0 Temp:  +34.0°C
Core1 Temp:  +38.0°C

k8temp-pci-00cb
Adapter: PCI adapter
Core0 Temp:  +32.0°C
Core1 Temp:  +36.0°C
```

Different hardware will display different temperature readings. For instance, the previous code is from an HP ProLiant server whereas the following output is from a ThinkPad laptop:

```
$ sensors -f
acpitz-virtual-0
Adapter: Virtual device
temp1:      +134.6°F  (crit = +260.6°F)
temp2:      +132.8°F  (crit = +219.2°F)
thinkpad-isa-0000
Adapter: ISA adapter
fan1:        3756 RPM
temp1:      +134.6°F
temp2:      +122.0°F
```

As you can see in the second output, we not only got a fan speed, we also were able to see what temperatures were considered critical for a device. This example added the -f option as well, which will convert temperatures into Fahrenheit for you.

So, what do you do if your server is running too hot? For starters, examine the airflow around the server and make sure the vents in and out of the server aren't clogged with dust. If the servers are in a datacenter that forces cool air from the bottom of the rack, you may want to consider moving particularly hot servers down closer to the floor (even if the servers aren't in such a datacenter, the air is likely to be cooler closer to the floor). If you have room in your rack, also consider spacing your servers out more so none are stacked on top of each other. If you have the bad habit of not rack mounting your servers but instead installing a shelf and stacking servers one on top of the other, that will also contribute to poor airflow and overheating.

Power Supply Failures

The final hardware failure this chapter will briefly cover is the power supply failure. Most modern server hardware has the option of having redundant power supplies so that if a power supply fails, the server stays up. Although complete power supply failures can be a problem, there really isn't that much to troubleshoot there—the power supply shuts off and stops working. The power supply failure briefly mentioned in this section is one in which the power supply still technically works but can't supply enough power.

When a power supply can't supply adequate power either due to being underpowered or because it is going to fail soon, it can cause strange problems on the server. In fact, the symptoms are much like RAM errors, in that programs can randomly crash, but bad power supplies can also cause temporary failures in hard drives. In your syslog, you may see either SMART errors or possibly you may experience a file system error that causes your system to remount in read-only mode (Chapter 4 covers this type of error in more detail), yet when you do a RAM check or a follow-up SMART check, things come up clean. Many administrators, when faced with this kind of issue, just assume the motherboard or some other core component is starting to fail, and they will toss out the whole server!

So how do you tell when problems like this are caused by a bad power supply and not by bad RAM or failing drives? Generally, when a power supply starts to fail and can't supply sufficient power, you'll notice problems are more common when a system is under heavy load. For instance, you may notice you start getting more frequent file system errors when your build server is in the middle of a big build (although this may also point to a cooling issue as well). The simplest way to diagnose this kind of problem is basic troubleshooting: Swap out the power supply with a new one (or one from a known good system) and see if you can re-create the issue.

Index

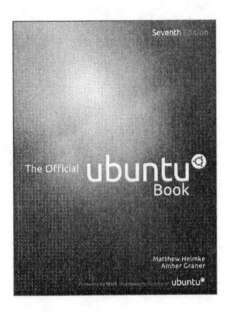